THE GENTLE ART OF
INTERVIEWING AND INTERROGATION
A Professional
Manual and Guide

THE GENTLE ART OF

INTERVIEWING

AND INTERROGATION

A Professional
Manual and Guide

Robert F. Royal
Steven R. Schutt

PRENTICE-HALL, Inc.   Englewood Cliffs, N.J.

Prentice-Hall International, Inc., *London*
Prentice-Hall of Australia, Pty. Ltd., *Sydney*
Prentice-Hall of Canada, Ltd., *Toronto*
Prentice-Hall of India Private Ltd., *New Delhi*
Prentice-Hall of Japan, Inc., *Tokyo*

This publication is designed to provide accurate and
authoritative information with regard to the subject matter covered. It is sold with the understanding that the
publisher is not engaged in rendering legal, accounting, or
other professional advice. If legal advice or other expert
assistance is required, the services of a competent professional person should be sought.

*... From a Declaration of Principles jointly adopted
by a Committee of the American Bar Association and
a Committee of Publishers and Associations*

Library of Congress Cataloging in Publication Data

Royal, Robert F
    The gentle art of interviewing and interrogation.

    Includes index.
    1. Interviewing in law enforcement. 2. Police
questioning. I. Schutt, Steven.R.,   joint
author. II. Title.
HV8073.R73   364.12'8   76-10285
ISBN 0-13-351247-9

Printed in the United States of America

A WORD FROM
THE AUTHORS

This book will increase the proficiency of professional interviewers and interrogators, federal, state and local law enforcement
officers, prosecutors, defenders, judges, legislators, personnel interviewers and directors, insurance examiners, and anyone involved in
or concerned about the art and mechanics of questioning for the
purposes of exploring or resolving issues.

Effective interviewing and interrogating is an art. It requires not
just a mechanical rundown of questions to elicit certain facts, but
the application of skills and techniques usually gained only after
years of experience.

In addition, it requires an understanding of human bias and
organism conditioning and a responsible recognition of the inter-
play of socio-psycho events that take place during an interview.

Therefore, this book goes beyond a simple cataloging of what to
do during an interview, interrogation or any meeting between two
or more people to discuss a specific matter.

It adds a new dimension to the technical literature on the
subject. It details the factors that govern an individual's providing
information; it defines and analyzes the mechanics of questioning
and the physical and psychological influence factors that directly
bear on creating the state of mind or rapport—the breakthrough—
that subsequently gains information. It gives you techniques for
gaining information in a humane way, yet information that the
individual is almost powerless to stop the flow of, even if aware

9

that the techniques are being used ... all of this while guaranteeing that the rights of that individual are not infringed upon.

Most important, this book will help minimize false judgments. How can this happen? Consider the following set of events taking place during an interrogation:

- the subject is unwilling to give information which is against his self-interest or which challenges his wellbeing.

- Once the subject's barriers are circumvented (by whatever means), then, as a general rule, there is no restraint to further revelation by the subject; the inhibition of self-interest has been momentarily removed.

- the subject will then discuss what is to him, at that moment, reality.

- reality has many variables within its structure. These variables may be collateral or motivating circumstances, and they are very sensitive to any controls exerted by an interviewer/interrogator.

- knowledge that a person commited an antisocial or overt act may not be, in and of itself, sufficiently informative to decide a social course of action toward that individual.

- in order for truly equitable social judgments to be made, a total picture of motivations and collateral or directly related events is vital.

- by his mere presence, the interviewer/interrogator asserts control over the eliciting of information regarding a total picture, and the values and subsequent judgments derived from the interview may be based on the biases of the interviewer/interrogator and not on the needs of the subject.

What consequences may stem from false judgments?

If an investigator is mistaken about a set of facts and mentally acquits a suspect, then perhaps that suspect may never be tried. This is a clear example of the distortion of a main fact regarding an overt act.

But what of motivations or collateral events? Can it be possible that courts somewhat base their judgments on the prejudices of law enforcement officers, rather than the needs of society? Is the personnel interviewer objectively fitting the applicant to the job, or are his judgments merely an externalization of his own set of values or prejudices?

This book will not get into lengthy philosophical discussions of morality in an attempt to answer these questions. Instead it will provide a practical, ethical, yet effective approach to achieving the same ends. By combining professional interviewing and interrogation techniques with heightened social awareness and a knowledge of organism manipulation into an understanding of human bias, false judgments will be minimized. Coupled with the added benefit of constant judicial scrutiny of the mechanism of interviewing and interrogation, perhaps we can achieve the much sought after "justice for all."

In addition, it's important to point out, to all those who would apply them, that the techniques which follow are not only benevolent, but efficient—based on more than 50 years of our combined experience in the field. For example, during the past 5 years more than $25,000,000 in confessions have been taken from individuals involved in crimes of money and property. Of that, nearly $14,000,000 in cash, securities, and stolen property has been recovered directly due to the application of the methods described in this book. The cases involved ranged from a $5,200,000 theft of product to a $20 register shortage.

And so, while the foremost aim is to achieve a socially responsible approach to systematic persuasion in arriving at the truth in any given issue, the techniques described in this book have also proven themselves to be uniquely effective in decades of actual use.

Robert F. Royal
Steven R. Schutt

We would like to express our special thanks to Sanford E. Beck, Esq., for having contributed the chapter entitled "Proof of Loss"

CONTENTS

A Word from the Authors . 9

1 Interviewing and Interrogation . 21

   A. Defined . B. What's Missing in Current Practice . C. An Approach to Meaningful Systematic Persuasion

2 The Mechanics of Questioning . 29

   A. Working Tools . B. Composition of Questions

3 Preparatory Work . 51

   A. The Defining of Unknowns . B. Aids and Auxiliaries . C. Location of Interview or Interrogation

4 Pre-Interview . 61

   A . Rapport . B. Exhibited Formality and Hostility . C. Order of Interviewing . D. Image of the Interviewer

5 Physical Influence Factors . 73

   A. Introductory Statement . B. Smoking . C. Alcohol . D. Drugs . E. Coffee and Tea (Caffeine) . F. Fatigue . G. Hunger and Thirst . H. Age . I. Sex

6 Recognition and Use of Psychological Factors . 81

   A. Importance . B. Psychological Factors

7   **How to Conduct Inquiries and Interviews . 95**

A. Important Considerations . B. Inquiries . C. Orient the Witness . D. Explore the "Unknown Details" . E. Cross-Examination . F. Detect and Explore Clues of Additional Information . G. Test Assertions . H. Summarize and Verify the Testimony . I. Draw Inferences and Conclusions from the Interview Results . J. Handling Unfriendly Witnesses . K. Pre-Employment Interviewing . L. Pre-Promotional and Transfer Interviewing . M. Systems and Operational Interviewing . N. Interviewing Women

8   **How to Interrogate . 115**

A. Why Do Suspects Confess? . B. Pre-Interrogation Considerations . C. Undermine Suspect's Confidence of Success . D. Offer the Suspect a Mutually Acceptable Solution . E. Make Submission Tolerable . F. Encourage Acquiescence and Pursue Indicators of Compliance . G. Consolidate Accomplishments . H. Interrogating Suspects of Questionable Guilt

9   **Emotional Inroads . 133**

A. The Father or Respected Figure Image . B. Normal Personality Insecurity

10   **Breakthrough . 143**

A. Defined . B. The "Buy Signs" . C. The Bluff . D. Furnishing Relief . E. Re-Establishing Stress . F. Dangers of Overconditioning

11   **Evidence . 155**

A. Classifications . B. Admissibility and Weight . C. Relevancy and Irrelevancy . D. Materiality and Immateriality . E. Competency and Incompetency . F. Other Tests of Admissibility . G. Judicial Notice . H. The Burden of Proof . I. The "Hearsay Rule" and Its Exceptions

12   **Basic Statements . 175**

A. Introduction . B. Types of Statements . C. Testing Assertions . D. Safeguarding

13   **Proof of Loss . 189**

A. Introduction . B. Objectives . C. Development and Preparation of a Confession Supporting a Fidelity Insurance Claim

14   **Ethics and Standards . 219**

A. Attitude . B. Insight and Awareness . C. Biases or Prejudices . D. Civil Liberties . E. Standards and Professionalism . F. Professional Ethics of Interviewing and Interrogation

Appendices . 229

Index . 236

1

INTERVIEWING AND INTERROGATION

1

INTERVIEWING AND INTERROGATION

A. DEFINED

Man is known by what he says and by what he does. The spoken word is potentially the largest source of the various forms of evidence available to the investigator. Further, it is the greatest verifying factor utilized in personnel interviewing. Usually, a criminal or quasi-criminal investigation cannot be completed until all the witnesses are interviewed and suspects are interrogated. Other forms of evidence are, of course, most important, but invariably testimony of witnesses and admissions of suspects bear heavily on the solutions of most investigations.

Let's agree on the definition that an interview is a meeting between two or more persons to talk about a specific matter. This would encompass interrogation, that is, the art and mechanics of questioning for the purpose of exploring or resolving issues. The concept of interviewing is associated with a more informal atmosphere. In this book, both terms (interviewing and interrogation) will be used interchangeably.

B. WHAT'S MISSING IN CURRENT PRACTICE

All too frequently, testimony which could have been developed, whether or not factual, is missed because of ineffective interviewing technique. A recent study of job applicants who were reinterviewed showed that an estimated seventy-five percent (75%) were rejected based on information the applicants had furnished at the time of the initial interview. Large sums are spent yearly by industry and business in lie-detector (polygraph) screening of applicants. The vast majority of people knowledgeable about the polygraph have consistently stated that in the area of employment applicant screening, most of the derogatory information is developed prior to the instrumentation phase of the interview. We can conclude that this is the result of a lack of understanding of the true role of the polygraph and poorly defined objectives of the original interview. Many organizations have developed a dependence upon pre-employment polygraph testing as the only approach to screening of employment applicants. In some states, restrictive legislation against pre-employment polygraphing has been enacted due to the legislators' belief that applicants' rights have been abused in their states. The real purpose of the polygraph is that of a truth-verifying device; yet, we have observed its use as a substitute for effective interviewing.

Humans represent the most complex life form; we have to be taught the ways and means of understanding behavior. Without this knowledge, the interviewer will lose contact, leading the subject to a diversion of the interview into topics of his own choosing. This, of course, leads to an interview which is unproductive, and it is one of the main causes of ineffective interrogation.

We note that in applicant interviewing, wherein the subject's cooperation is highly exhibited, there is often an inability to acquire all the pertinent available information. This situation may be explained by our basically puritanical social orientation, which may cause friends, family, and associates to report things only reflective of their conscious moods. They usually avoid any conversation detrimental to their own self-interest. Inexperienced interviewers attempt to develop derogatory information by appealing to family relationships, loyalty, and religion. This form of motivation is seldom more than moderately effective and, even then, only with people who are personally acquainted with the interviewer. The criminal and quasi-criminal situation quickly shows the illogical nature of such methods. Even in normal conversation between long-term friends, the discussions are usually limited to areas of mutual interest, but fail to explore all details of a matter in an objective manner. Should one touch on any of the other's bias areas thereafter, the perimeters will be defined and the conversational theme will shift. To interview or interrogate successfully, a number of physical and mental influence factors must be assembled in a logical sequence and applied to the subject efficiently so as to obtain information which may be against his self-interest.

May we point out that most interviewing and interrogation is a product of the mentor method, wherein the apprentice learns the mistakes of the master. This is not an indictment of trial and error methodology, but obtaining any degree of skill by these means alone will require years of practice. Such time spent in practice usually results in extremely costly reduction of performance, due to errors in judgment and procedure. Virtually anything learnable through trial and error can be learned through systematized study, more rapidly and more thoroughly.

There are a large number of do's and don'ts cited by authors writing about interviewing; however, there seems to be little information as to why the do's and don'ts exist. Even more apparent is the lack of a formalized guide for the application of such rules. There are those who would relegate interviewing and interrogation to the development of an artful intuition; that is to say, "You must develop your intuition and let it guide you on how to proceed with each subject."

Intuition is merely a judgment that has come to the surface with supposed spontaneity. In reality, it is derived from precedent and observations of similar situations. It has the shortcomings of permitting a conclusion without total evaluation of all variable factors. Moreover, if situations encountered are not within the limits of previous experience, then all that is left is a disguised guess.

We do not dismiss the development of highly-skilled interviewers when innate skill and sufficient experience are possessed. Failure to recognize and define interviewing and interrogation, however, as logical systems of organism conditioning is another of the inadequacies of the current training media.

C. AN APPROACH TO MEANINGFUL SYSTEMATIC PERSUASION

This book will not replace experience. It can, however, most certainly decrease on-the-job training time and effectively increase the ultimate degree of proficiency available to the interviewer or interrogator. One of the objectives of this work is to explore organism conditioning and the factors governing its application.

There are some who would suppress the printing of this knowledge, perhaps out of fear that anyone who reads it might be beyond effective interviewing. We contend that, even though the subject may be armed with knowledge of these techniques, he would be almost powerless in stopping the flow of information.

Others might object to the discussions of conditioning, stress, and emotional inroads as synonymous to "brainwashing." To this we reply that, although most anyone can be made to confess to virtually anything given sufficient time, there is still an extremely fine line between persuasion and psychological duress. There is also a gray zone between early states of suggestibility in hypnosis and repetition in salesmanship. Knowledge of these boundaries will undoubtedly provide the legal checks and balances necessary to safeguard the rights of the individual.

Our legal system is concerned with the overborne will of a person who makes admissions against self-interest. Systematic persuasion, which is conducted in an amiable and humane atmosphere by the interviewer, should in no way conflict with our legal system. We concede that physical or mental abuse will usually result in the gaining of information against the subject's self-interest. Humane motives aside, the main reason our legal system has progressed from physical and mental cruelties is that we have reached a level of sophistication enabling us to reason that a subject will furnish false information to stop any physical or mental discomfort. Any interviewers who have need of such methods are certainly sadistic, uninformed, and incompetent. Within the framework of the United States Constitution and those of most other countries where the legal systems derive from English Common Law, the investigator is morally bound to protect the rights of the individual and, equally, the public interest. There are *no* circumstances that will justify the interviewer's violation of those rights.

There are some persons in law enforcement who believe the protection of a person's rights is a hindrance to effective investigation. We shall see in succeeding chapters that the guaranteeing of the rights of the individual is actually more of an aid to the investigator than a hindrance.

The real objective of interrogation is the exploration and resolution of issues, not necessarily the gaining of an oral or written confession. Even the subject's false statement could be very helpful to the interviewer, or later on to the investigation, because the subject who lies is then committed to the psychological defense of a fantasy, the antithesis of reality. The latter is finite, whereas fantasy is a total variable; hence, it is evident that those committed to deception will work harder to maintain their defense. No man can be in all places at once; reality will obviously seep through.

2

THE MECHANICS OF QUESTIONING

2

THE MECHANICS OF QUESTIONING

A. WORKING TOOLS

1. Language or Speech

If the subject does not speak the same language as the interviewer, it will be necessary to use an interpreter. Even when both parties are familiar with the same language, the subject may have speech or hearing difficulties. Such problems can usually be overcome by speaking loudly, requesting the subject to wear a hearing aid or to write the questions and answers. If the subject can neither speak nor write, it may be possible to find an interpreter who can converse with him by sign language. Do not be deceived by a subject who acts as though he does not understand or talk coherently. It is not uncommon for suspects or witnesses, immigrants in particular, to pretend an inability to comprehend. Be careful of your conversations in their presence; if possible, make inquiries of persons who would know the subject's ability to understand the local language. In some cases, the pretense may be discovered by deliberately carrying on a planned discussion in his presence about a matter of much concern to him, while casually observing his facial expressions and other signs of reaction.

2. Words and Expressions

Be sure that both you and the subject completely understand the words and manner of speech to be used during the interview. Trade terms, local expressions, uncommon words, speech accents, and even sentence construction may result in a misunderstanding. Try to talk at the level and use the speech mannerisms of the subject to the extent necessary for him to understand. If there appears to be any doubt about definitions, they should be immediately explained and clarified so that both you and the subject have the same understanding.

3. Conduct and Appearance

Your conduct, appearance, facial expressions, and body actions can often be effectively used to influence the subject. The interviewer should watch continuously for, and carefully analyze, any such reactions by the subject. Agreement, disagreement, or a neutral attitude may all be indicated by a nod of the head, a shrug of the shoulders, or a gesture with the hands. An emotional state may be revealed by a facial expression, a smile, a laugh, a wink of the eye, an inflection or tone of voice, the context of what is said, tenseness of body, etc.

4. Attitude

The attitude of the subject can frequently be deduced from a combination of, and changes in, the factors cited above. For example, a sneering facial expression would indicate a hostile attitude.

5. Influence

You may use these same factors to help influence the subject. A smile or a pat on the shoulder may impress him with your friendliness. Your tone of voice may indicate to him that you are sympathetic. A skeptical facial expression may indicate that you do not believe his contentions.

B. COMPOSITION OF QUESTIONS

1. Communication

One must be able to communicate effectively with the subject in order to have a productive interview. Limited information will be obtained if the subject does not respond to inquiries or his answers are not understood.

Speech is the principal means of communication, but impressions received through the other sensory organs are most important. Good communication requires, under all conditions, the use of the entire mind and body. It not only involves what is said or done by one participant, but also includes how it is sensorially perceived, understood, and reacted to by the other party. Conversation passes through fluctuating conditions that change with each new perception. The deliberate speech and behavior expressions of each party are intended to influence the attitude or actions of the other participant.

If the interviewer can perceive expressions, interpret their significance, and apply appropriate influences more effectively than the subject, he will exercise considerable control over the subject's attitude and actions. This is one basis for successful interviewing and interrogating.

The communication process is so fundamental in interviewing that efficiency is essential. Some of the more important efficiency factors which one must learn to use are discussed in the following section.

2. Questions Are Tools

Questions are the principal tools of interviewing. The quantity and quality of information obtained from suspects and witnesses will usually be proportional to your skill in formulating and asking questions.

The word "question" has two general meanings:

a. That which is asked

b. The act of asking

In interviewing, we use the word "questioning" or the term "to question" as meaning both that which is asked and the asking process.

In general, you use speech for the purpose of persuading the listener to take some action, change his attitude, or acquire a different state of feeling. When you use speech in the questioning process, your primary objective is to induce him to talk and give information about the matter under investigation. In addition to seeking information, you may use the questioning process to test, perplex, confuse, or psychologically entrap the subject. Cross-examination is an example of this.

3. Characteristics of Good Questions

Words are the basic units the interviewer uses to convey thoughts and persuade. In speech, you must know the effect desired before uttering the words calculated to achieve it. The effect obtained will be limited by your choice and arrangement of words. In interviewing, the nature of your questions and persuasions will follow your pattern of thinking. Most questions or assertions are based on assumptions, and it is highly essential that the assumptions not be based on faulty information.

Some of the fundamental characteristics of good question construction are:

a. Make the questions short and confined to one topic.

b. Make the questions clear and easily understood.

c. Avoid the use of frightening or super-realistic words; such as confession, murder, forger, dope addict, embezzler, etc. Use milder terms.

d. *Use precise questions.* A precise question is one that calls for a specific or an exact answer. It limits the requested answer to a definite item of information. For example, the following questions are increasingly precise in a progressive order:

   i. What did you do?

   ii. What did you do when you were growing up?

   iii. What did you do last year?

    iv. What did you do yesterday?

    v. What did you do yesterday afternoon?

    vi. What did you do about 3:15 yesterday afternoon?

    vii. What did you do about getting home when you missed the 3:15 bus yesterday afternoon?

Precise questions are important. They tend to bring precise answers; they help keep the discussion and the pattern of thinking moving toward a particular goal. Usually, they will bring forth the desired information quickly and with minimal effort.

e. *Use discerning questions.* Discerning questions are questions designed to produce information directly bearing on the matter under discussion. They are questions that discriminate between what is relevant and what is irrelevant.

4. Important Types of Questions

a. *Extended answer questions*

Questions should generally be framed to require a narrative answer. Soliciting "Yes" or "No" answers usually restricts the information that the subject may be inclined to give and is often inadequate to answer completely the inquiry being made. They are also frequently leading or suggestive. Questions requiring a "Yes" or "No" answer may be acceptable when summarizing or verifying information, and even most desirable during cross-examination, but they should not be used when seeking new information.

b. *Leading questions*

    i. Suggest the desired answer; or

    ii. Assume something to be a fact which has not been established as fact; or

    iii. Embody a fact and require a simple negative or affirmative answer.

Leading or suggestive questions tend to influence the answers given by a subject and should be avoided while asking for original information.

Such questions do have value, however, to test or fracture previous assertations, or should you wish to get a particular answer, or to refresh the memory of a subject.

Examples of suggestive questions in order of their suggestiveness:

   i. Did you see a _____?

   ii. Didn't you see a _____?

   iii. Didn't you see the _____?

   iv. Wasn't there a _____?

c. Questions or statements involving "double or triple negatives" are confusing and often suggest an answer opposite to the correct one. They should not be used under any circumstances:

   i. *Didn't* he have no dinner?

   ii. He *couldn't hardly* stand up.

   iii. He *never* said *nothing* to *nobody*.

   iv. *Couldn't* you see him *neither?*

   v. He *didn't* do it, I *don't* believe.

   vi. *I couldn't barely* hear him.

   vii. *Didn't* you *not* stop at a stop sign before entering the intersection?

d. *Complex questions.* Complex questions and statements are those that:

   i. Are too complicated to be easily understood.

   ii. Cover more than one subject or topic.

   iii. Require more than one answer.

   iv. Require a complicated answer.

A classic example: "Illumination is required to be extinguished before these premises are vacated," instead of saying, "Put the lights out before you leave"; or "What did you do with the package and how much did you pay for the delivery truck?" instead of asking two separate questions.

Complex questions and statements should be avoided. They serve no useful purpose. They tend to confuse the subject and frequently lead to unintended false answers.

e. *Attitude questions.* The attitude of the interviewer can be conveyed by question or statement construction, as well as by the manner of asking. When you desire to influence the mood of a subject, you should use both construction and manner of expression to achieve the goal.

Examples of friendly questions and statements:

 i. How are you this morning, John?

 ii. Do you like sports?

 iii. Have a cigarette.

 iv. Would you care to tell me what you did Saturday?

Examples of stern questions and statements:

 i. Don't lie to me!

 ii. You can't have a drink now.

 iii. Do you expect the jury to believe that?

 iv. You had better explain your actions.

Most questions can be composed from the seven "W's." The following seven interrogative words are useful as a basis for a high percentage of interviewing and interrogating questions:

 i. What? (What happened?)

 ii. When? (When did it happen?)

 iii. Where? (Where did it happen?)

 iv. Why? (Why did it happen?)

 v. How? (How did it happen?)

 vi. Who? (Who was involved?)

 vii. Which? (Which one did it?)

The questions "Why?" and "Why not?" are the most powerful and are of the greatest value in interrogations. You will usually find that when you have been asked and acquired complete answers to these seven "W's" the issue being explored is satisfactorily resolved.

These seven "W's" are so basic to the investigative art that by learning to use them as a memorized key, one has the outline for all information to be obtained in any type of inquiry, interview, or interrogation.

f. *Question sequences. Issues are generally resolved by sequences of questions.* In both interviewing and interrogating, your efforts are directed toward resolving the questionable issues. As a rule, it requires a sequence of questions to resolve each issue. *An issue is an occurrence, situation, or object, in an investigation, that needs to be explained or resolved.*

The sequence of questions should focus on the issue. Each question must push your solution effort in a particular direction:

i. *General to specific sequences.* The most efficient means of resolving an issue is to have the questions converge on it by progressing from **General** to **Specific** in construction. Seek general information on the setting of an event before exploring *details*. Place the suspect at the scene before inquiring into his acts *there*. Determine the act before *exploring* how or why it *was done.*

The following example illustrates inquiring into an investigative issue by progressing from "general to specific." The interview up to this point has revealed that money was divided among some thieves. The next issue to be probed is: "Who got a share of the money and how much did each get?"

Question: How was the money divided?
Answer: At a meeting.

Question: Where did this meeting take place?
Answer: In Joe's Bar.

Question: How many were there?
Answer: There were five of us.

Question: Who were they?
Answer: Well, Joe, Pete, Fred, Mike, and me.

Question: How was the dividing done?
Answer: Joe split it up into five piles.

Question: How much did each of you get?
Answer: I don't know—Joe didn't count the money.
             He just guessed at the size of each pile.

Question: Did you all get the same size pile?
Answer: No. Joe and Pete did more on the job, so
             they had twice as big a pile as the rest of us.

Question: Do you know how much was in your pile?
Answer: Yes. I counted it when I got home. I had
             just a little over $900.00.

Question: Based on the size of the piles, you and Fred
             and Mike got about $900.00 each and Joe
             and Pete got about $1,800.00 each?
Answer: That would seem about right.

In this example, the location of the act (dividing the
money) was established first, the participants were then
determined, and the method of dividing was ascertained, followed by details that permitted estimating
the amounts. If we refer back to the issue, we see that
it has been resolved in depth and we have acquired the
answers sought.

ii. *Reaching backward.* Your questions will progress more
    logically with less risk of omissions if use of transition
    to connect thoughts is applied. To do this, start with
    known information and work toward areas of undis-
    closed information. An efficient method of achieving
    this type of sequence is to reach backward mentally
    over the known information and frame the next ques-
    tion as a logical continuation of the facts previously
    related.

    The following illustration portrays use of the **Known to
    Unknown** sequence procedure by reaching backward
    for orientation before proceeding to the next question
    in each instance. **The statements that are underlined**

and enclosed in parentheses are the unspoken thoughts of the questioner as he prepares to frame each new question:

Question: (You said earlier you went to Mudville.) Now, what means of transportation did you use?

Answer: A car.

Question: (If you went in a car?) Who drove?

Answer: I did.

Question: (You drove a car to Mudville.) Was anyone with you?

Answer: Two guys went with me.

Question: (You drove a car in which there were two passengers.) What were their names? Etc.

iii. *More specific estimates of quantities.* You will rarely get the right answer the first time you ask for the number or quantity of anything. To determine more specifically quantities of time, space, and material, the following type of question sequence may be of value— "CHANGE OF REFERENCE POINT" to localize measurements. When descriptions of quantities are complicated, they frequently can be simplified by changing the reference point.

Examples:

a. A witness may describe the location of an incident that occurred as four miles east, one and one-half miles south, two miles southeast, and three miles west of town. It is difficult to comprehend exactly where this location is. If guided, the witness may be able to simplify the description of the location by advising that it is one-half mile west of the Mudville Town Hall.

b. It does not mean much to the average person for a witness to talk about seven containers full of heroin. If the witness will convert the amount to ounces, pounds, or injections for an addict, it gives a clearer picture of the quantity.

iv. *When description of quantities are vague or indefinite*, they can often be made more specific by comparing them with similar items of known quantity. Examples:

a. Was he taller than I am?

b. Which one was the biggest?

c. What share of the loot did you get?

d. In some cases where quantities are persistently given in generalities, it is productive to bracket the probable amount by suggesting exaggerated or minimized quantities, and by enlarging or subdividing the suggested quantity to get the witness to agree more specifically on an amount; i.e.—

Question: How far away was Smith when you first saw him?
Answer: He was a long ways down the road.

Question: About how far would you say?
Answer: I don't know—quite a ways.

Question: Do you know how long a mile is?
Answer: I'm a pretty good judge of distance.

Question: How far would you say it is from here to City Hall?
Answer: About two miles.

Question: That is a good estimate. Now, would you say Smith was more or less than a mile away when you saw him?
Answer: Much less.

Question: Was it more or less than a quarter mile?
Answer: More, I think.

Question: Would you say it was closer to a quarter-mile, or more nearly a half-mile?
Answer: It was closer to a quarter-mile.

Question: Then, would it be correct to say the
              distance was a little more than a quarter
              of a mile?

Answer: That would be about right.

Don't outsmart yourself with oversimplifications, as in
the following anecdote:

During direct examination, a witness to a railroad
accident established that he was present on his porch
approximately a half-mile from the scene of the accident, and that the accident occurred at night. On
cross-examination, counsel asked, "How far can you see
at night from your front porch?" Witness answered: "I
don't know!" The counsel, seeking a point which he
might use to discredit the witness's testimony, pro-
ceeded, "What do you mean, you don't know?" With
that, the witness answered, "How far is it from my
front porch to the moon?"

v. *Controlled-answer questioning techniques.* Controlled-
answer questions or statements may be used to stimulate a desired answer or impression, as follows:

a. To stimulate a person to admit that he has knowledge about some matter, such as: "I understand you
   were present when the liquor was delivered, so would
   you please describe what happened?" This provides a
   stronger incentive to admit knowledge than merely
   to say, "Were you present when the liquor was
   delivered?"

b. To stimulate the person to agree to talk or give
   information, such as: "If you are not involved in
   this, I'm sure you would not mind discussing it with
   me, would you?" This is a much stronger incentive
   to cooperate than to say, "Do you have any objection to telling me what you know?" Always avoid
   using a question that has a negative construction
   when making a request such as, "Would you refuse
   answering a few questions?" A personnel man should
   avoid asking such a question as, "You never have

been arrested, have you?" (In effect, he would be suggesting a "No" answer.)

5. The Three Principal Procedures for Applying Questioning Techniques

a. *Free narrative* is an orderly, continuous account of an event or incident given with or without prompting. It is used to get a quick resume of what a subject knows or is willing to tell about a matter. Usually, it can be initiated by requesting the subject to tell what he knows about the matter. Be sure to designate *specifically* the occurrence to be discussed.

Frequently, the subject must be controlled to keep him from digressing. Use a minimum of interruptions, and do not be too hasty in stopping him from wandering in his narration. He will sometimes give valuable clues while talking about things that are only partially related to the matter under investigation. Be careful not to erroneously interpret deviations from the *anticipated* information as "wandering."

b. *Direct examination* is systematic questioning designed to bring out a connected account of an event or an incident. Its purpose is to elicit new information or to fill in details omitted during free narrative:

  i. Begin by asking questions that are not likely to cause the subject to become hostile.

  ii. Ask the questions in a manner that will develop the facts in the order of their occurrence or in some other systematic order.

  iii. Ask only one question at a time, and frame the questions so that only one answer is required by each question.

  iv. Ask straightforward and frank questions—no bluff, no tricks, and no shrewd approaches.

  v. Give the subject ample time to answer—do not rush him.

vi. Try to help him to remember, but do not suggest answers and be careful not to imply any particular answer by facial expressions, gestures, method of asking questions, or types of questions asked.

vii. Repeat or rephrase questions if necessary to get the desired facts.

viii. Be sure you understand the answers, and if they are not perfectly clear, have the subject interpret them at once.

ix. Give the subject an opportunity to qualify his answers.

x. Separate facts from inferences.

xi. Have subject give comparisons by percentages, fractions, estimates of time and distance, types of automobiles, recognition of persons, etc., to ascertain the accuracy of his judgment and assertions.

xii. Get all of the facts. Almost every subject or witness can furnish you with additional information beyond what was initially provided.

xiii. After the subject has given his narrative account, ask questions about every item discussed. Ask questions about little things, and the answers will frequently contain clues to previously unreported information of interest.

xiv. Upon conclusion of the direct examination, ask the subject to summarize his information, and then follow-up by a resummarization of your own and have the subject verify the correctness of the conclusions.

c. *Cross-examination*, on the part of an interviewer, is exploratory questioning conducted for the purpose of testing previous testimony for correctness, resolving conflicting information, determining completeness, filling in evaded details, evaluating the judgment of witnesses, and undermining the self-confidence created by deception.

In so far as is practicable, all previous testimony should be evaluated and checked against known or readily available information. This will give clues to portions of testimony that should be further explored during cross-examination, such as:

i. Attempts to evade answers.

ii. Vague answers.

iii. Conflicts of information.

iv. Inconsistent answers to the same or similar questions.

v. Apparent falsehoods or inaccurate information.

vi. Suspicious actions of subject.

Cross-examination should never include loud, abusive, or "third-degree" methodology. The investigator should generally act friendly, but reserved and unemotional. Effective cross-examination can always be conducted without abusing the subject.

Have the subject repeat testimony about a particular event or occurrence several times. Attempt to keep expanding on details at random, without following a definite order or sequence. This is usually best accompanied by asking about it in a different manner from time to time. Ask what happened, why it happened, when it happened, who was there, why they were there, how did they come to be there, and what preceded or followed the event. Occasionally, insinuate a different context or relationship of details; e.g., initial question—"When did you first meet Mr. Jones?" The first subsequent query would be: "Tell me what led up to your first meeting with Mr. Jones"; which might be followed by a second subsequent question, "Did Mr. Jones give you any indication of his plans prior to the previously mentioned meeting?" The natural third subsequent query would be: "How long after you learned of Mr. Jones' plan did the indicated meeting take place?" etc. Be alert for inconsistencies in his replies. If he is recalling facts, he will usually be consistent. A deceptive subject generally finds more and more lies are necessary as additional details are required, and he either forgets what he has previously asserted or fabricates details that are not compatible with previous statements.

It is permissible to use suggestive questions and inferences during cross-examination (such as, "You saw John Doe strike his supervisor, did you not?" "You had no trouble seeing Richard Roe in the bright moonlight?" "Would you estimate the distance to the still to be about one mile?" "Wouldn't you say that only an expert could manipulate a set of books this well?") If the subject is fabricating information, he will frequently concur in suggested answers to fill in details of his story. If many of the questions are designed to suggest false answers, the subject may be trapped into false assertions that can be shown to be erroneous. (This procedure may be valuable in testing the validity of testimony from witnesses, as well as in undermining the confidence of deceptive subjects in their ability to outwit the interviewer.)

Ask about known information as if it were unknown. Use a casual tone and demeanor. Show no sign of surprise or emotion when false answers are given.

Ask about unknown information as if it were known. Use facial expressions and tone of voice that would subtly convey the impression of cunningness or trickery. Slyly make the subject think that you expect him to lie or that you are daring him to lie. Use good judgment in selecting questions that have a strong probability of affirmative, truthful answers. If you score on several correct guesses and are cautious, the subject may be greatly concerned and influenced by what he thinks you know. Remember, it is not what you know but what the subject knows that will furnish the solution.

Specifically explore vague or evaded sections of testimony or confessions. Frequently, such areas of information are purposely slighted because they are particularly embarrassing or detrimental to the subject. Always be suspicious that these slighted details are of direct and important concern to the subject. Often they involve some previously undisclosed information that pertains to him.

Point out conflicts. It is usually best to ask all questions that stimulate deception before confronting the subject with evidence of conflicts or proof of falsehoods. This will give him a chance to build up a large number of lies before he realizes that he has been led into a trap, and will more completely undermine his confidence when he realizes the deception has been discovered. Ask the subject to explain inconsistencies or conflicts in his statement. Inform him as to how his statements are proven false by previously established facts, physical evidence, contradictory circumstances, etc. Ask for an explanation. Any explanations or revised information given by a subject should be subjected to the same direct cross-examination scrutiny as was afforded the original story.

Point out physical signs of lying; such as, nervousness, guilty appearance, dry mouth, sweating hands, etc. This procedure frequently gives the subject great concern and helps to undermine his confidence of escape.

Rationalize with the subject. Ask him to imagine that he is an investigator, a judge, a juryman, or a citizen. Then, point out the items of evidence, one at a time, asking him after each item if he wouldn't be convinced of lying or guilt if he had to judge these items. (For example: "If you were the jury, what would you think if you heard a man say that he couldn't remember his associate's name?" "What would you think if a man said he hauled a truckload of goods to a remote farmhouse twice each week but had no suspicions that it was being used to violate the law?" "What would you think if a man stated he had never been in a farmer's field but you were shown his boot and a plaster cast of a print made by this boot in the field?" Etc.)

Summarize the known facts and compare them with the subject's statements.

Then, point out the only logical explanation—an explaining away of damaging evidence; next, point out how illogical his answers are.

d. *How To Use an Interpreter in Questioning*

When using an interpreter in interviewing or interrogating, it is important that he be fluent in the exact dialect spoken by the subject. Merely learning a foreign language in school is usually not enough. It is also unsatisfactory to use a person who has a poor command of English.

The interpreter must know your language well enough to understand exactly what you wish to convey. He must have a sufficient vocabulary and knowledge of sentence structure in both languages to make an accurate translation. He must be able to pass on to the subject the information, as well as reflect the attitude and manner of expression you wish to convey. Further, he must be able to recognize any idiosyncrasies in the subject's answers and bring them to your attention, along with the reply information.

A male interpreter is generally preferable, as the status of women is considered inferior by men in many foreign countries and a female interpreter may be resented.

If the interpreter is a foreigner, be sure he is not from the same area as the subject, to avoid any personal element, such as friendship, prejudices, or common interests.

The subject should generally be seated in a chair opposite you, with the interpreter in between but slightly to one side, so that by merely turning his head he directly faces either you or the subject as the conversation switches back and forth.

It is desirable to orient the interpreter prior to the questioning as follows:

 i. He should merely act as a vehicle for accurately interpreting and passing the information back and forth between you and the subject.

 ii. He should imitate your voice inflection and gestures as much as possible.

 iii. There should be no conversation between the interpreter and the subject, other than what you tell him to say.

iv. No matter what the subject says, the interpreter should pass it on to you, rather than evaluate its worth himself. This includes even the most trivial remarks or exclamations.

v. Even if the subject has some knowledge of English, if you have decided to use an interpreter, you should pass all information through the interpreter to avoid confusion as to whom the subject should answer.

You must completely control the interpreter and, through him, control the subject. Usually, you are restricted to use of the more routine methods of interviewing or interrogating because of the limitations of the interpreter. At the conclusion of the questioning, after the subject has left the room, it is often worthwhile to ask the interpreter how he evaluates the subject.

In spite of the limitations and difficulties involved in using an interpreter, you can often conduct very successful interviews and interrogations if they are well planned and controlled.

3

PREPARATORY WORK

3

PREPARATORY WORK

A. THE DEFINING OF UNKNOWNS

The first consideration in planning for the questioning of witnesses or suspects is whether or not this is potentially the most valuable means of getting the desired information under the existing circumstances. There are a number of investigative processes that are effective in procuring information from people, as follows:

1. Interviewing

2. Use of confidential sources and informants

3. Undercover

4. Surveillance

5. Surreptitious listening

6. Interrogation

7. Other

Frequently, existing conditions may suggest that one of the other investigative processes would be more productive than interviewing or interrogating. (For example: When the contacting of witnesses and suspects might tip off the violator and cause him to flee or be more cautious.)

In almost every case, it will be desirable to question every person thought to have information before the case is completed, but there will be times during an investigation when such questioning is not advisable. You must select a time when the questioning is advisable. You must select a time when the questioning of a particular person will be beneficial and not harmful to the investigation. When questioning does appear in order, give careful thought to the alternative investigative procedures and methods.

You must attempt to locate and eventually process *every* suspected violator and *every* witness who may have relevant information. In many cases, there will not be adequate evidence to convict the violators unless all sources of information have been exhausted. In other cases, you cannot be sure that you have identified all of the associates or conspirators in a crime and can prove the exact participation of each, until all possible information has been obtained and evaluated. Sometimes a single statement from what appeared to be the least important witness will change the entire complexion of a case. There is also the possibility that the unquestioned witness or suspect may unexpectedly appear in court for the defense and testify to matters that are completely strange to you. If you have previously taken a statement from him, you will be aware of, and can prepare for, the additional defense testimony; or if he completely changes his statement, you may be able to impeach him.

Initially, suspects may be developed by ascertaining whose actions, whereabouts, reputation, or motives are questionable in relation to the violation. Similarly, witnesses may be identified by determining who was in a position to have observed worthwhile information through sight, hearing, feel, or smell; and ascertaining who performs services, receives reports, or maintains records of value. Even a person having only hearsay information is worth interviewing for clues to more suitable sources. When known witnesses or suspects are being questioned, they should be queried about others who may be involved or have information.

If there are no apparent witnesses or suspects, it is sometimes productive to interview all people who live in the crime scene area, or interview the types of merchants who may have furnished the supplies for a criminal activity, or interview transportation companies who may have provided transportation to or from the area for the violators, or interview pawn shops where stolen goods may have been sold and other similar groups that might be in a position to have knowledge.

In some cases, it is productive to question past violators of crimes with a similar modus operandi. A check with other law-enforcement agencies handling similar types of crimes is often productive in locating suspects.

Before engaging in interview or interrogation, you should orient yourself as completely as possible in the details of the case and the background, character, and habits of associated witnesses and suspects. This will help in appraising the subject's character and in determining the most effective questioning procedures applicable to that particular individual, as well as providing some facts to use as controls and levers during the questioning. Some of the sources of background information are:

1. Read all available investigation reports and talk to any other investigators who may have preceded you on the case.

2. Examine statements already taken.

3. If practicable, visit scene of crime.

4. Evaluate all related circumstantial evidence.

5. Examine any related physical evidence.

6. Procure and examine any previous criminal record of suspects and potentially hostile witnesses.

7. Check telephone directories, city directories, and similar readily available sources of information about the addresses, occupations, families, etc., of involved witnesses or suspects.

8. In some cases, it may be of value to make inquiries of local police officers, a postman, local storekeepers, neighbors, etc., before questioning an individual.

It is impossible to complete efficiently and directly any task unless you know what you are trying to accomplish. It is essential that you have a clearcut goal or objective that can serve as a target toward which plans and efforts can be directed. There are two distinct factors to be considered in determining an interviewing or interrogating objective:

First, determine the requirements of the law or investigative assignment. In criminal cases, the requirements are ascertained by analyzing the law involved and identifying the elements that must be proven. In non-criminal cases, you should carefully analyze the problem to be investigated and identify the matters to be explored.

Second, determine the "unknown details" to be resolved. Ask yourself, "Why should I question this individual?" The reasons for questioning a person may be many or few; they may be strong or slight; but there should be a reason, and you should be able to comprehend specifically what that reason is. Some common reasons are:

1. He was on the scene when the crime was committed.

2. He lives or was present in a neighborhood where he might have heard or observed something.

3. Other investigation indicates he has knowledge or is involved.

4. His handwriting, personal effects, or fingerprints were found at the crime scene.

5. He has committed similar crimes.

6. He had a motive or an opportunity to commit the crime.

7. He is associated with or knows a great deal about the probable events.

8. He maintains official records or processes information that may be of value.

9. Other.

When you have decided on the probable relationship of the individual to your case, you are in a position to judge what details he is likely or apt to know. Each "unknown" is in effect a question you want an answer to. Therefore, you should write down the "unknown" points in the form of questions arranged in logical order. Be sure to include several or more questions of a general nature to ascertain if the subject has knowledge on unanticipated matters.

These "unknown detail" questions should cover every topic you wish to discuss. As a rule, they will indicate the topic to be resolved, but will not specifically cover the individual questions that must be asked to resolve the topic. During the discussion of an "unknown," you may need to ask a number of questions before it is resolved or explored to your satisfaction. In fact, you may not ever ask the topic question at all.

Following is an example of typical "unknown detail" questions that might be explored during an interview or interrogation of a chauffeur who reported that the company car was stolen from the curb while he was delivering mail in another building:

1. *What* is the total identity of the driver?

2. *What* is the description and identification of the car?

3. *When* did the theft take place?

4. *Where* did the theft take place?

5. *Why* was he at that place?

6. *How* did the theft occur?

7. *What* precautions, if any, had been taken to prevent the theft?

8. *Who* else has any personal knowledge of theft?

9. *How, when,* and *to whom* was the theft reported?

10. *Who* can verify any parts of the driver's story?

11. *Does* the driver have any suspicions regarding the perpetrator of the theft?

12. *What* is the driver's background, driving record?

13. *Was* any property of value in the car when it was taken?

14. What else does driver know of significance?

B. AIDS AND AUXILIARIES

Aids and auxiliaries are important in both interviewing and interrogating. They are things that will be useful to the investigator during the questioning of a witness or suspect. Their value, however, depends on their being available in the proper form when needed.

You should carefully ascertain the existence of potentially useful aids and auxiliaries and be sure to arrange for their availability in advance. Some typical aids and auxiliaries are:

1. Written or recorded statements of other witnesses and suspects.

2. Photographs of suspects, crime scenes, and evidence.

3. Lineup to identify suspects.

4. Contraband or instruments of a crime.

5. Other suspects or witnesses to be confronted.

6. Background information.

7. Information from other sources that is to be verified or discredited.

8. Previous statements of same subject.

9. Results of laboratory and expert examinations.

10. Polygraph instrumentation.

11. Recording equipment and/or stenographer.

C. LOCATION OF INTERVIEW OR INTERROGATION

You must evaluate and attempt to control the physical conditions where the interview or interrogation will take place. If the local setting is not favorable, the simplest solution is to move to a new location.

It is generally desirable to interview in a location that is strange to the subject. However, friendly witnesses may be interviewed in their homes or offices if there are no disturbing or interfering situations present.

Almost without exception, suspects and unfriendly witnesses should be removed from familiar surroundings. Most persons feel more secure and, accordingly, more contented in their homes or offices. In addition, they feel a necessity to maintain personal integrity before family, friends, and neighbors. Removing a person from familiar locations eliminates these barriers and initiates the process of getting him into a submissive or "yes" mood. It also permits taking him to a location and atmosphere that is conducive to cooperation and truthfulness.

The location of an interview achieves its greatest importance from the fact that it is the setting that provides an indelible first image of the interviewer to the subject. Once that impression is formed, it remains as a platform for any interview. The home ground of the interviewer is a familiar place to him, but not so to the subject. Since fear is the direct reinforcement for defensive activity, it is then important to decrease his fears. A location that has a cheerful, "You have nothing to fear" quality about it can do much to break down pre-interview defensiveness. Many in the role of law-enforcement interrogators depend on the subject's fears to break him down. They will advocate the use of drab surroundings that are quite barren, in an effort to increase the subject's fear and the feeling of "What is going to happen to me now?" The use of fear and anxiety as motivating forces for obtaining information are to be objected to. Use of a bare, gray-walled interrogation room is tantamount to a modern-day "star chamber."

With respect to the preceding remarks on barrenness, drabness, and bare walls, many proponents of these methods hide behind the idea that anything present during an interview extraneous to the necessities of the interviewer will distract the subject. Some of the largest commercial confessions of recent times have been taken under conditions that directly refute this idea. This is not to say that distracting influences should not be kept to a minimum. What is meant is that if one has a regular interview environment, it should have enough cheerful coloring to dispel fear. When the interview room is shoddy, then the interviewer may be opposed by the subject's concept of him that spells shoddiness. If that image is what the interviewer is trying to project, *well and good.* However, when that is not what the interviewer wishes to project, then he must work that much harder to offset it. Visual distractions are to be avoided. Now, let's define visual distractions!

Try to avoid locations where noise, activity, or surroundings will distract. The room should be private and the furniture, comfortable. There should be no glaring lights or signs of restraint. Generally, exclude friends and relatives.

A personnel man whom I knew had a glassed-in enclosure for an interview area. The glass looked out on a manufacturing facility. When the interviewee was seated, he could see most of the production areas in the plant. The personnel man told me that he constantly felt he was losing control of the interview. I asked if subject distraction was the answer. The apparently simple addition of drapes completely eliminated the problem. What was distracting the subject was the movement of plant activity. Basically, that is visual distraction in a nut shell. I can recall interviewing under abominable conditions, but the most distracting thing I have ever come across is movement within the peripheral vision of the subject. The more obvious non-moving distractions are pictures that do not have a restful theme, and unshaded windows.

Subjects are usually distracted by audible sounds above a muted level; therefore, it is most desirable for the interview location to be quiet. One of the most successful interrogators I have ever known refused even to begin an interview unless he had a location that guaranteed quiet. This is the main reason that telephones should be excluded from interview rooms. Quiet during a criminal or quasi-criminal interrogation is of even greater importance, because the subject will, of necessity, be involved in more mental effort to attempt deception.

When an interview is conducted away from the interview room, such as on-the-scene interviewing, problems can be kept to a minimum if the basic rules of audio-visual distractability are followed. Pick a quiet place. Seat the subject so as to preclude as much visible movement as possible. If, for example, the investigators' cars are at the location of an accident, and the investigators are interviewing witnesses or participants, then the investigator doing the interviewing should park his vehicle in such a manner as to keep the subject from viewing the accident scene and as much movement as possible.

4

PRE-INTERVIEW

4

PRE-INTERVIEW

A. RAPPORT

Rapport is a necessary ingredient to be developed between the subject and the interviewer, from the outset of the interview. This embodies an understanding between the two individuals and conveys a sense of identification on the part of *both* persons, plus the ability to communicate.

There is a natural inclination for most people to be formal with each other, particularly those who are not close friends. This feeling of formality may appear in the form of skepticism and reserve at first meeting. At times, the formality does take on the appearance of hostility. Under the existence of these conditions, you can see, it would be most difficult for anyone to furnish a degree of cooperation or information. Most interviewees, witnesses, and suspects feel apprehensive about giving derogatory information, regardless of whom it would concern. Resistance to the disclosure of such information is considerably increased if the interviewer is a total stranger, or if something is not done to establish a friendly and trusting attitude on the part of the subject. Once rapport is established, you have begun the "yes" attitude.

The following devices are recommended:

1. Identify yourself.

2. Begin the discussion by commenting on a topic of apparent interest to the subject.

3. Establish confidence and friendliness by talking for a period about everyday subjects. In other words, have a "friendly visit."

4. Keep conversation informal and easy.

5. Display pleasant emotional responses and avoid unpleasant expressions.

6. Urge the subject, but never try to hurry him.

7. Do not ask questions that lead a witness or subject to believe that you are suspicious of him, either by composition of the question or by method of asking.

8. Appear interested and sympathetic to his problems.

9. Do not begin the interview or interrogation until the subject appears to be quite friendly and cooperative.

10. Try to re-establish rapport at any time during the questioning if the subject appears to become reserved or hostile.

An interrogation cannot be successful unless the subject is induced to converse. You can persuade the most reluctant subject or witness to become conversational if sufficient patience is applied. Be alert for signs of hostility.

Prior to any interview, a personal history should be developed covering the subject's background, character, and basic attitudes. Have subject furnish his full name, place and date of birth, and his present and one or more previous addresses; get names and addresses of relatives, plus names of friends and associates (if applicable), education, employment, etc.

We note that the interviewer usually obtains clues to the subject's attitudes and character in reviewing his present and past life.

B. EXHIBITED FORMALITY AND HOSTILITY

The subject may exhibit formality and/or hostility due to:

1. General fear of the situation

2. Subjective fear of the interviewer

The asking of questions in our daily associations with people is so common that we consider the process as almost instinctive and let it go as that. Spontaneous inquiries that are adequate for the ordinary curiosities of life are quite inefficient for getting concealed information or for breaking down general and subjective fears. Further, to tell a subject, "You have nothing to fear" often may result in the subject's expression of general fear.

Primitive man spent little time in planning the building of his simple and unsophisticated shelters. However, modern housing requires extensive planning and preliminary preparation to satisfy the wants and needs of the present-day man. Successful interviewing and interrogation needs the support of proper planning and preparation.

To break down the general fear in any situation, the investigator must conduct an objective study of the individual's defensive attitudes and the fears from which they were formed, *prior* to beginning the interview. By the subtle placement of fear-reducing statements within the framework of the interview, these defensive attitudes can be greatly neutralized. To exemplify: An employment applicant usually has fear of the discovery of some petty falsification in answering the questions presented on the application, such as, the inflating of previous earnings, etc. The applicant may also be fearful that he is not physically appealing or that he is not the best-dressed person who may be applying for the job. These general fears can be removed by employing a sales technique commonly referred to as "taking the wind out of the prospect's sails." Realizing that the applicant has these fears, the interviewer would state at the very beginning that "I am (he is) aware that there are minor or 'little' discrepancies appearing on your application; however, I do not really care about them because we know the reasoning of our applicants, etc." An applicant's insecurity which is motivated by his general dress or physical appearance can be dealt with by complimenting the color of his tie or the degree of his suntan, etc.

The interview phase may differ from the interrogative phase because these general fears are linked to the objectives of the interrogation; and, therefore, alleviation of these general fears is dependent on the rapport developed by the interrogator.

The subjective fears of the interviewer are a very real thing caused by both physical characteristics and projection of traits within the personality of the interviewer. Since the personality is another way of saying "the total conscious behavior" of the individual (and the conscious behavior can be influenced), then it is important that the interviewer develop those traits which will combat personal fear and project an image which will subdue individual defensiveness.

C. ORDER OF INTERVIEWING

Generally, witnesses who can and will voluntarily give the most complete account of the event and associated background information should be interviewed first. This will give you an early overall insight into the matter and provide information of value to be utilized in processing the other witnesses and suspects.

Suspects and hostile witnesses should generally be questioned last in order to take advantage of the information gained from the cooperative witnesses. Generally, interrogate the suspects thought to be "easiest" prior to interviewing the more difficult ones.

In some cases, it is advantageous to question several witnesses or suspects simultaneously or at alternate intervals during the same time period, for the purpose of "playing" one person against another or to facilitate any calculated use of bluffs, staged situations, or the taking advantage of natural distrust which often exists among witnesses early in an investigation.

Neither interviews nor interrogations should be initiated unless there is sufficient time available to permit an extended period of questioning without undesirable interruptions.

As a rule, friendly witnesses should be interviewed as soon after the occurrence as possible. If practicable, it is often desirable to interrogate a strongly suspected person while he is still under the emotional stress of a crime and before he has had an opportunity to fabricate a false story or alibi. In some cases, a suspect's conversation or mannerisms will indicate that he is unusually emotionally disturbed about a crime, and immediate interrogation should be initiated. If a suspect cannot be interrogated at once, it is usually advisable to wait until all readily available background information relating to him and the occurrence has been assimilated.

D. IMAGE OF THE INTERVIEWER

1. Personality

To be truly proficient at interviewing or interrogation, one must possess the ability to portray a great variety of personality traits. The need to adjust character to harmonize with, or dominate, the many moods and traits of the subject is necessary. The interviewer/interrogator requires greater histrionic skill than the average actor. He may become so involved in the part that he plays that he will actually feel the emotions and attitudes he exhibits. The interviewer must be able to pretend anger, fear, joy, and numerous other emotions without affecting his judgment or revealing any personal emotion about the subject.

2. Sympathy

Let's define sympathy as "to be in accord, to give understanding, to give consolation, and to agree." These are all definitions of sympathy, and they all piece together that part of the interviewer's projected image that we call the "sympathetic personality." We are discussing interviewing and interrogation, and not attempting to change therapeutically the personality of the interviewer. Certain irrevocable changes will have to occur, however, for the interviewer to master his art. The qualities of a sympathetic personality are such that one might do well to develop them as a normal disposition.

3. Sincerity

Subjects are like children in that they can sense insincerity and sham. Sincere sympathy is vital to the interviewer. Once the subject discovers that he has been lied to, all the technique in the world will not remake the interviewer's shattered image. Rapport will be lost. Moreover, it will be almost impossible for another interviewer to regain the subject's confidence and establish his (second interviewer's) own rapport with the subject. Insincerity is a form of lying that can be fatal to any interview or interrogation. To be sincere and to project sincerity are quite different. We must project sincerity to be successful in interviewing/interrogating.

4. Impartiality

Impartiality, complete neutrality, and openmindedness are yet other components of the projected personality image. The interviewer who pronounces judgments prior to the obtaining of information may well defeat his own purpose. There are cases where the interviewer or the interrogator is a spokesman for society. Yet, he cannot voice his views or concepts of morality during the interview. Were this to occur, the image of neutrality would shatter and the subject would feel that the interviewer had something to gain. The subject might very possibly feel threatened.

5. Empathy

The subject requires understanding. All that has been said about the fears he is accumulating would tend to indicate that the only way to gain that understanding would be to empathize with him. To say, "I understand your problems," is not enough. The subject must be addressed with a genuine understanding of his individual problems. Put yourself in his place—not only on viewing the situation from his side of the fence, but through his eyes as well. This will give you some idea of the understanding he seeks. Look at your own fears and defenses when in his situation. Ask yourself, "What would relieve my fears?" The use of empathy, or projection of one's own self into the subject's problem, will create such an aura of understanding that the interviewer's image will be that of an almost infallible being. This is often referred to as the "bedside manner" of the doctor, or the "charm" of the politician, or simply as "charisma."

6. Firmness

The interviewer must also project firmness. At various points during an interview, you will note that the very personality of the subject attempts to seize control. This will usually occur by a testing of the interviewer's own personality. Any sign of weakness on the part of the interviewer, under these conditions, may compromise the interview and put the subject in the driver's seat, so to speak. Frequently, the female applicant sensing the man's awe of femininity will use this tool to attempt to gain control of the course of the interview. The most common form of attempt to seize the lead is the "stipulation." The subject will attempt to set down a system of ground rules which he wishes followed. He may say, "I will answer any question about 'X,' or 'Y,' or 'Z,' but not others." At this point, if firmness is not displayed, the entire image of the interviewer is shattered. A compromise could preserve the situation and still project firmness. An example would be: "I will ask no questions that do not bear on the matter at hand, but I am the one who knows what is pertinent to our discussion." Another common method of seizing control is a show of indignation for the very need for an interview. Logic and an honest explanation of objectives usually overcome indignation.

Incidentally, these various attempts to seize control are very good indicators of the defensive attitudes and fears that are being built by the subject. They may also reflect to some extent the possible involvement of the subject in the situation. They are also measures of the amount of compulsion the subject must exert to relieve himself of guilt feelings.

Firmness is not arrogance. Most people interviewed or interrogated are not "on the outs" with society. The authors have personally noted several instances where witnesses stated they would not cooperate further because they felt they were being treated as common criminals. The crown of authority that sometimes rests with an interrogator is close to arrogance. Certainly, the interviewer/interrogator cannot be defensive at any point, but it should be stressed that being firm, or "taking a tough track," or "being hardnosed" is not arrogance. Firmness is best described as "a sales approach with a definite objective." Never lose sight of the objective of the interview or interrogation, no matter what the technique used to gain an individual point. Always come back to the necessary approaches that lead to the objective.

An interviewer must discipline himself by adhering to the following guidelines:

a. Do not prejudge anyone.

b. Subdue all personal prejudices.

c. Keep an open mind, receptive to all information regardless of its nature.

d. Try to evaluate each development on its own merit.

e. Learn to refrain from trying to impress the subject, unless such action is used as a specific device of questioning. We have noticed this to be a common fault among interviewers and interrogators. They will conduct themselves and ask questions in a manner designed to impress the subject with their importance. This is often created by the interviewer's exhibiting sarcasm, anger, disgust, and other acts which lessen the interviewer's image to the subject. The interviewer should always suppress his own emotional attitudes and apply all his faculties to the objective of the interview.

f. In some cases, the use of deception, such as staged events or bluffs, may be acceptable. However, there can be no justification for deliberate lies or false promises. Even the implied false promise is unethical and hardly more than a veiled manner of saying that the end justified the means.

g. Never underestimate the mentality or physical endurance of the subject. On occasion, it may exceed your own. The specialized training that you receive should enable you to interrogate or interview almost any individual. Always maintain the supposition that the subject may be highly intelligent, and adjust accordingly.

h. Do not take on contemptuous attitudes (unless they are used as specific questioning devices), such as:

   i. Never sneer.

   ii. Don't ridicule.

   iii. Don't bully.

   iv. Do not belittle the subject, his position, or information derived.

   v. During the course of general conversation, avoid such controversial issues as religion, racial matters, and politics, if at all possible.

   vi. Do not make promises that can't be kept.

   vii. Be fair.

viii. Never consider the gaining of information or a confession as a victory. This in itself may be a "stepping stone" toward the total objective.

i. Try not to show signs of personal nervousness, such as pacing around the room.

j. The subject must believe that your only motivation is a search for truth. Avoid the impression that your only interest is information or a confession.

k. Never raise your voice. The moment you do, you have endangered the interview.

l. Try to avoid antagonizing the subject.

m. Display total confidence in your course of action.

n. Be a good listener.

o. Be patient.

p. *Be gentle. You can always get tough after being gentle, but you can never be gentle after being tough.*

q. *Be persistent.*

5

PHYSICAL INFLUENCE FACTORS

5

PHYSICAL INFLUENCE FACTORS

A. INTRODUCTORY STATEMENT

The body and brain of the human being function as a single coordinated unit. Any physical condition of the body will influence the mental acitivity of the brain. They are integrated to the point that each is dependent upon the other for functional needs.

The brain depends on the circulatory system for food and waste elimination.

All information is transmitted to the brain through the sensory organs.

The results of brain activity can generally be expressed only by muscular or vocal activity.

The activity of the brain is influenced by existing conditions of the body, as well as by anticipation of future physical influences.

Current and anticipated physical conditions are frequently controllable or can, if necessary, be neutralized to the advantage of the interviewer/interrogator. Some of the influences that the interviewer can control are as follows.

73

B. SMOKING

Smoking decreases both physical and mental efficiency of the human organism. On those occasions when it is desirable for the intellect of the subject to be dulled, smoking should be encouraged.

Observation of the rate and changes-of-rate of smoking may be indicative of the subject's anxiety level, as well as fluctuations in his current emotional state. Since under some situations smoking offers emotional release, it may be desirable to have the subject refrain from smoking when attempting to preserve a state of high emotional pitch.

C. ALCOHOL

Alcohol is a cytological poison that produces ascending paralysis of the brain and nervous system. Any appearance of stimulation while drinking alcoholic beverages is due to the removal of some of the subject's inhibitory power. The ascending order of alcohol absorption is shown in the following list of symptoms:

1. A feeling of wellbeing.

2. Exultation.

3. Increased self-confidence.

4. Loss of judgment.

5. Loquaciousness.

6. Dulling of the senses.

7. Loss of skill.

8. Slurred speech.

9. Disturbance of equilibrium.

10. Visual disturbance (color, motion, and distance perception).

11. Apathy.

12. Tremors.

13. Sweating.

14. Dilation of surface capillaries.

15. Cessation of automatic movements.

16. Stupor.

17. Coma.

18. Death (4% to 5% alcohol in the blood).

In the early stages of intoxication, there is a marked decrease of self-control and a weakening of willpower. During any form of interview or interrogation, the use of any alcoholic beverage or intoxicant cannot be condoned. If, in the course of a criminal or quasi-criminal proceeding, a subject is found to be intoxicated, then it would be desirable to delay actual questioning until he is sufficiently sober to be aware of his constitutional rights.

Although intoxicated persons show a reduced ability to fabricate deception, they also show sensory impairment and reduction of reasoning power, as well as decreased judgment. On this account, the interviewer should be extremely cautious of any testimony obtained from persons under the influence of alcohol.

D. DRUGS

The opiates, including opium, morphine, and heroin, together with other painkilling synthetics have a depressant effect on the body.

Cocaine, amphetamine, and other central nervous system stimulants cause a feeling of exhilaration, quicken the intellect, and give the user considerable fluency of conversation. These symptoms are generally followed by a feeling of depression.

The barbituates—chloral hydrate and other hypnotics—are sedative-type drugs that show a general depressant effect on the system.

Tranquilizers and hallucinogens exert widely divergent systematic effects, but maintain one common denominator—that being a distortion of reality, as the user knew it, prior to the administration of the drug.

There can be no reason for the use of any drugs in legitimate interviewing or interrogation. When a person is under the influence of drugs, all questioning should be delayed until the subject has reached a state of mind close to that which preceded the drug use.

E. COFFEE AND TEA (CAFFEINE)

The caffeine in coffee and tea acts as both a physical and mental stimulant. Caffeine delays the onset of fatigue, and the mental-physical processes of a subject can be increased as much as 4% by the consumption of even a moderate amount.

During cross-examination or formal interrogation, subjects should not be offered caffeine-bearing beverages. However, during personnel interviews or contacts with friendly witnesses, the use of these beverages may increase the subject's mental alertness and aid in the stimulation of memory in providing more detailed information.

F. FATIGUE

Fatigue results from the accumulation of waste deposits which decrease the efficiency of the body. Strenuous exercise and extensive physical activity, loss of sleep, or *strong emotions* are all contributory factors to the generation of fatigue. Recovery from fatigue occurs only as waste products are cleared from the blood or additional energy producers are carried to the cells. Fatigue produces increased resistance to nervous system activity. Mental inhibitory processes are also affected by fatigue and tend to release responses that are ordinarily held in check. This condition will often make the subject more receptive to persuasion and less shrewd under cross-examination. During interrogation, although it may be desirable to foster fatigue in order to lower the subject's resistance to "win points," we recommend that you do nothing to induce fatigue deliberately.

G. HUNGER AND THIRST

The discomforts of hunger and thirst are distractions which interfere with both the interviewer and the subject. A general rule should be that both the interviewer and the subject have adequate food and nonalcoholic beverages before the interview.

Incidentally, one of the most important rapport-forming fear-breakers is the act of subject and interviewer eating together at the same table or in close proximity. In observing the behavior of lesser primates, we note that, although monkeys will fight over food, when food is evenly distributed, monkeys *never* fight while eating.

During a cross-examination or interrogation, we note, the subject's energy level will be reduced by selection of food and beverage that are very high in protein and low in sugar and fats. The physiological result is that the normal person experiences a considerable time delay in obtaining food energy. The slow breakdown of protein being digested also produces the condition of fatigue.

The authors do not recommend that the interviewer utilize high-protein fatigue inducers. Our courts may take judicial note of some of these physiological subtleties during a proceeding, and thereby reaffirm existing law or provide new guidelines for interviewing.

H. AGE

1. *Children* frequently make good witnesses. However, information from children should be cautiously obtained and carefully evaluated. In some matters, children are much more observant than adults, but they are not always capable of differentiating between that which was seen and that which was heard. A vivid imagination may create distorted or false information. The ability of children to make better observations than most adults exists because their senses are more receptive to what they see and their minds are less preoccupied. Their greatest shortcoming stems from the lack of experience which would allow for a discriminate or correct interpretation of what is observed. The result is that they have not learned the meaning of, the nature of, or the understanding of language or expressions being used.

As a rule, children are quite susceptible to suggestion. They will adopt the expressions of others or respond with answers that they believe are desired, rather than relating only fact. For these reasons, the abilities and reliabilities of children acting as witnesses should be tested. Such tests should consist of inquiries with parents, teachers, etc., to ascertain traits and reliability. Ability to understand and evaluate information may be tested by asking irrelevant questions requiring perception and judgment similar to the observations being reported. Always attempt to find out who talked to the child about the matter prior to your doing so. Obtain the comments or instructions received from those persons who have conducted the previous interview.

Children often tire quickly and should not be questioned when fatigued. Waiting until other sources of information are available, and checked, can also help to evaluate the testimony of the child.

Because of the extreme susceptibility to suggestion and the desire for approval, it is always desirable and probably a good rule of thumb to record stenographically or by tape-recorder any interview of young children.

2. *Old people* are much like children in their susceptibility to suggestion. There are also the matters of poor eyesight, poor hearing, bad memory, delusions and hallucinations which might affect their testimony. It is best not to depend too heavily on the unverified testimony of the aged, unless the above factors can be accounted for.

I. SEX

Men and boys usually make better witnesses with respect to mechanical things, such as, automobiles, airplanes, etc.

Women and girls frequently are more informed about social matters and the petty intrigues of the neighborhood (gossip). They are interested in people and their surroundings and often are better witnesses than men with regard to the activities, dress characteristics, etc., of persons and with respect to furnishings, furniture arrangements, and similar conditions in the living quarters of homes or other buildings of direct interest to them. Women and girls are sometimes more emotional and less reliable with respect to matters of an emotion-producing nature.

6

RECOGNITION AND USE OF
PSYCHOLOGICAL FACTORS

6

RECOGNITION AND USE OF
PSYCHOLOGICAL FACTORS

A. IMPORTANCE

There are a number of psychological factors that have a bearing on interviewing and interrogating procedures, as well as affecting the reliability of the information obtained. It is highly desirable to ascertain the existence or nature of such factors in order to better evaluate the information obtained. In some cases, the investigator can influence or control these factors to his advantage.

B. PSYCHOLOGICAL FACTORS

Following are cited some of the more important psychological factors:

1. The Emotions

The emotions of primary concern to the investigator are anger, fear and neutral excitement. They involve mental and physical processes which prepare the individual to meet an expected emergency. Physically, they are largely identical, but a definite mental distinction exists. The interviewer can frequently control the type and strength of the emotion generated.

During *anger,* the individual has resolved to meet the emergency by resisting, including physical combat if necessary. Anger against the investigator is usually undesirable in a subject who is being interviewed or interrogated. Anger directed against confederates, an unfaithful spouse, a betraying friend, etc., may be helpful during questioning.

Anger against the interviewer can usually be avoided by greeting the subject in a friendly manner and creating the impression that the investigator is in no way responsible for the subject's current or past difficulties.

The festering of anger in the subject against other persons or situations can be achieved by accentuating their danger or harm to the subject or his possessions.

During *fear,* the individual tends to seek escape. This may be accomplished either by physical flights or by removal of the immediate emergency through abandonment of resistance and development of a willingness to resolve the matter through cooperation and truth telling. The fear emotion is usually beneficial when interviewing hostile witnesses or interrogating suspects. When attempting to get detailed testimony from friendly witnesses, fear should be pacified.

Fear is aroused by any present or imagined danger. Fear is not aroused until it develops that an individual knows enough about a situation to realize the potential danger but is not able to resolve the difficulty satisfactorily.

Fear will develop spontaneously in a suspect if he is confronted with a serious difficulty, is frustrated in all attempts to evade it, and is aware that the solution may result in unpleasant consequences. If a suspect is convinced that he cannot evade the solution and that the answer provided may result in unpleasant consequences, or if the suspect is convinced that he cannot evade the consequences of his acts, he will frequently develop sufficient fear to make him receptive to suggestions of *escape by confessing.*

Fear can be reduced or eliminated by removing the real or imagined difficulty, or by finding a solution which the individual can accept.

In *neutral excitement,* the individual is merely prepared to meet whatever may arise. Neutral excitement is of some concern to you in that it affects the perception of the witness and may develop into fear or anger with changes in mental attitude. It is generally aroused when the individual is aware of a potential danger not specifically directed at him. It may usually be removed by elimination of the danger or by developing familiarity with the cause.

Emotional conditions of the body are frequently incited by "habit" developed through repeated emotional reaction to situations of many kinds. This is called a "conditioned reflex" and exists in almost all persons with respect to lying and similar forms of deception. Most people exhibit some emotion whenever they knowingly tell a lie, no matter how small the untruth may be. Anger and excitement are likewise subject to a conditioned reflex excitation which causes them to appear habitually in response to emergencies or symbols of potential danger.

Physical symptoms of emotion (sometimes erroneously called "guilt" symptoms):

a. Dryness of mouth—frequent requests for water.

b. Restlessness—frequent change in position, tapping of foot, fidgeting, gripping arms of chair, elbows held tight to body, running hands through hair; chewing fingernails, pencils, or other objects.

c. Excessive sweating—particularly of hands or in armpits.

d. Unusually pallid or ruddy complexion—changes in complexion.

e. Pulsation of the carotid artery.

f. Excessive swallowing—indicated by the unusual activity of the "Adam's Apple."

g. Avoiding direct gaze of the interrogator's eyes.

h. Excessive assertions of truthfulness; such as, "I hope to die if I am lying"; or, "I'll swear that is the truth standing on my dead mother's grave"; or, "My right arm to God."

i. Evasive or vague answers; such as, "I am not sure what happened"; "I can't remember"; "I have forgotten"; "I don't think it could have been that much"; etc.

j. A disturbing feeling of tenseness and turbulence in the pit of the stomach.

2. Perception

Perception is the process of receiving knowledge through the sense organs—sight, hearing, smell, taste, and touch.

Most human behavior is in response to impressions received through the sensory organs, and any distortion of those impressions may affect the nature of the behavior. Defective eyesight, hearing, etc., may result in faulty interception of impressions. Pain, emotion, severe discomfort, exhaustion, etc., may distract the individual so that he becomes preoccupied and inattentive to ordinary impressions received through the eyes, ears, and other senses. Mental impairment may cause the senses to function abnormally and produce delusions or hallucinations.

Perception requires mental interpretation of the knowledge received by the sensory organs. Such interpretations are based on past experiences and reasoning power of the individual. (For example: A person would be unable to identify a type of dog he had never previously heard of, but would recognize the animal as a dog because it bears characteristics similar to other dogs he has seen.) This limitation of individual ability should be kept in mind when evaluating testimony of witnesses.

Visual limitations: Eye defects may frequently be evaluated by ascertaining the type and strength of glasses worn by a subject. Tests have roughly determined the following limitations on the distance at which persons can be recognized:

a. A well-known person in good illumination can, on the average, be recognized at a distance as far as 150 feet.

b. If a person has some physical, dress, or manner peculiarities, it may be possible to recognize him up to about 300 feet.

c. A person who is not well-known could not usually be recognized at more than 100 feet.

d. In bright moonlight, recognition is usually limited to about 30 feet.

It is estimated that approximately three percent of any population is color-blind.

Because of the sensory impressions and all of the variables involved in perception, we point out that human testimony can only be considered reliable when it is carefully corroborated or all assertions are thoroughly cross-checked.

In 1913, the German psychologist Dauber performed a classic experiment in which he showed 369 school children a picture of a small boy with brown hair, brown coat, blue trousers, and brown shoes. Thereafter, each of the children was asked to name the colors in the different parts of the picture.

The blue trousers were described:

By the Boys	By the Girls
15 times as blue	8 times as green
20 times as brown	19 times as brown
5 times as yellow	3 times as yellow
4 times as gray	7 times as gray
	3 times as red
	3 times as black

The brown coat was described:

By the Boys	By the Girls
28 times as blue	21 times as blue
18 times as green	12 times as green
13 times as gray	19 times as gray
20 times as red	9 times as red
2 times as yellow	

The brown hair was described:

By the Boys	By the Girls
35 times as black	12 times as black
2 times as light	2 times as light

Eighteen children described the brown shoes as black, and many claimed that the boy in the picture was barefoot.

Such experiments serve to illustrate the many pitfalls met in criminal investigations when a suspect is identified through an untrained witness.[1]

---

[1] Dauber, *Die Gliechformigkiet des Psychischen Greschehens und die Zeugehaussagen,* Fortschritt der Psychologie (1913).

3. Memory

a. *Principles of Association:* Whenever two things have been observed together, a subsequent recurrence of one will tend to bring back the other. (When questioning persons, encourage them to give unimportant details, as this will help them to remember the important aspects.)

The more frequently a thing is encountered, the easier it is to remember. (You can place more confidence in testimony regarding incidents that have been observed more than once by the witness. If a witness relates his testimony several times to an investigator, it will help him to remember the details should he be called later as a court witness. This procedure of the interviewer, of repeatedly taking testimony, should in no way be construed later as "coaching the witness."

The memory of an incident or observation decreases with *time.* (Talk to a witness as soon as possible.)

People usually remember the *first contacts* with persons, things, or incidents better than succeeding contacts. Therefore, be suspicious of witnesses or suspects who can remember complete details of an occurrence but cannot remember when, why, or how the incidents transpired or whose idea it was, and similar preliminary aspects.

Incidents that stimulate a strong emotion are more easily remembered, but less reliable as to details. (If an incident frightened or angered an individual, he will usually remember it, unless the lapse of time is great, but he may be quite inaccurate in reporting just what happened.)

An occurrence that has been largely forgotten can often be remembered in considerable detail if one pertinent incident can be recalled.

Frequently, the memory of a witness can be refreshed about an occurrence by injecting a name, date, place, or similar vague clue in your questioning. If no details are known to the investigator, the witness may be able to refresh his own mind by recalling, in detail, all incidents that might in any way have a bearing on or connection with the occurrence.

A prospective witness who at first denies knowledge of an occurrence may, with his memory refreshed, later provide useful testimony.

Individuals who have suffered a *head injury* or have been temporarily knocked unconscious may not be able to remember what occurred only a few minutes or hours prior to the injury.

If a person specifically *intends to remember* something, he usually can recall it in much greater detail than he otherwise would. When witnesses are first interviewed, they should be specifically requested to remember important aspects of testimony, should it later be needed for a proceeding.

A witness who remembers information received through one sensory organ particularly well may be quite inefficient in recalling information received through a different sensory organ. (An individual who remembers what he sees may be poor at remembering what he hears.)

b. *Older people* may develop an impaired memory. They frequently forget more recent things, but still remember earlier happenings.

People tend to fill in missing details with *imagined material.* This is particularly true when the recollections of the witness are faulty. Such witnesses usually find it difficult to distinguish between what is remembered and what is imagined. *The greater the gap(s) in a person's memory, the greater will be the tendency for the individual to fill in the gap with imagined details.* (Interview witnesses early, before these memory gaps develop, to assure more accurate testimony.)

4. Recognition

We recognize something by observing its strong similarity to something previously observed. (For example: We recognize a person because of a preceding memory of a person similar to him in his appearance and actions.)

Persons or things that are not known well are frequently subject to false recognition. (Never have a witness view a suspect unless he is concealed in a lineup of similarly dressed persons, to test the accuracy of recollection and reduce the possibility of suggesting an identity.)

Usually conditions surrounding persons or things may affect recognition.

If a suspect changes clothes, gets a haircut, removes his glasses, or similar changes are effected, a witness may be unable to recognize him. Therefore, always have persons or things in as nearly the original condition and situation as possible before being viewed by witnesses. (Compare apples to apples and oranges to oranges.)

5. Suggestion

Interviewers/interrogators have, through the act of suggestion, placed an idea before a person in such a manner that this person does not question the validity of the idea, and the interviewer may ask "loaded questions" in which the desired answer is suggested by the question. In their efforts to please, some witnesses and suspects will respond with answers which they feel are most pleasing to the investigator, *regardless* of the facts.

Individuals whose memory of an incident is faulty are often particularly responsive to suggestions as to the unremembered details. The investigator himself must be careful not to suggest speculative information which might be accepted and vouched for by a witness or suspect.

In some cases, a person will disregard his own observations and give information that is in accord with the majority opinion of other witnesses. People generally do not like to contradict or come into conflict with others and will, accordingly, adjust their own expressions to conform with the known testimony of others.

You must be careful to get the personal observations of an individual and not a considered opinion that may have been adjusted to agree with known statements of others. Try to talk to witnesses and suspects before they have been influenced by others; keep them separated during interview or interrogation; and, during the initial interview, do not suggest the position taken by other witnesses or suspects.

Other factors which may influence or suggest answers are:

a. Tone of voice.

b. Facial expressions.

c. General posture.

d. Gestures.

e. General surroundings. (A witness observing a suspect sitting on a bench with a group of known offenders may conclude that the suspect also is an offender.)

6. Bias

A person who is biased or prejudiced may unintentionally give distorted information.

An individual who strongly dislikes the use of alcholic liquors may conclude that a neighbor who drinks was intoxicated when he became involved in an automobile accident. If a witness hates a suspect, he is likely to report derogatory information about him and ignore favorable information. Be alert for signs of bias or prejudice which may color the testimony of a witness.

7. Submission

In any interrogation, both the interviewer and subject will find themselves engaging in what could be termed "a struggle." Interviewers and interrogators cannot allow any external force to be exercised which would compel the subject to submit to any ideas not of his own free will. If he ceases to struggle while he is still able to resist, *his submission is his own act.* Moreover, people have learned through most of their lives that submission may be an asset on many occasions, as it prevents them from wasting energy following impossible or impracticable courses of action. Usually, they yield without open opposition to persons whose positions so far outrank theirs that resistance seems futile (such as bosses, traffic officers, etc.). This tendency to submit to authority or superiority and cooperate with an investigator can frequently be exploited if the investigator creates an impression of his own personal eminence in the minds of the witnesses or suspect. Judges are seated on elevated benches to accentuate the eminence of their position.

In many respects, witnesses and suspects submit readily to an investigator because of the personal eminence he derives from his position. For example:

a. When they consent to accompany the investigator to the office or some other location.

b. When they peaceably submit to an apprehension or arrest.

c. When they consent to talk about the matter under investigation.

d. When, upon instructions, they sit in a certain place, stay seated, remain in a particular room, remain quiet, or talk only when requested, request permission to get a drink, etc.

It may be desirable to keep suspects and witnesses in this submissive, or "yes," mood. Act friendly, but do not be overly friendly. Do not be arrogant. Always attempt to anticipate how far a person will submit without rebelling. If skillfully handled, this submissive tendency can be a major incentive in motivating a witness to cooperate or a suspect to confess. When a subject shows signs of becoming antagonistic, he is losing his submissive attitude.

8. Deception

First we note the inclination to deceive, and later we note the abilities developed, as a most common trait among persons of all ages and cultures. Lying and other forms of deception are action patterns generally used to compensate for personal inadequacies. In most cases, such conduct is resorted to when the individual feels incapable or is unprepared to solve a problem by more desirable means. (The young child gains personal satisfaction by deceiving his mother and pretending to be asleep as long as the crib is rocked; some merchants try to achieve a financial gain by misrepresenting their merchandise; in war time, armies try to gain an advantage over the enemy by deceptive maneuvers.)

Also, the deceiver attempts to use deception as an avenue to escape from the consequences of his deeds.

The fear emotion and lying are corollary processes that are closely associated. When an individual is confronted by a danger which he is unable to overcome by ordinary means, he begins to develop fear which, in turn, prepares and motivates him for escaping from danger. This is called the "fight or flight mechanism."

When questioned, the suspect is usually not in a position to attempt physical flight, hence, he seeks escape through lying. One of the interrogator's goals is to convince the suspect that escape through lying is blocked, then offering him an acceptable solution which will include his cooperation.

7

HOW TO CONDUCT
INQUIRIES AND INTERVIEWS

7

HOW TO CONDUCT INQUIRIES AND INTERVIEWS

A. IMPORTANT CONSIDERATIONS

An interview is defined as a meeting between two persons to talk about a specific matter. In investigations, it usually includes visiting and questioning for the purpose of resolving or exploring issues. It is generally somewhat informal and friendly.

As a rule, neither witnesses nor suspects will cooperate well unless they are aware of some authority to question them. In the absence of such authority, they are inclined to evade questions because of the attitude that you have no right to question them and they are not obligated to answer. It is, therefore, important to reveal your authority to investigate that particular matter prior to requesting information. People are more impressed with what they believe than with what they see, so always get them to believe the reason for the interview.

A witness is any individual other than a suspect who possesses or is in control of, information having value in a matter under investigation. Friendly witnesses are usually initially motivated by a desire to be sociable. They usually present no problem except that of controlling their cooperation; however, care must be exercised not to alienate them during the questioning. *As a rule, time means money to the average witness; and, insofar as practical,*

95

you should try to arrange interviews when the witness is not busy, endeavoring to complete the interview as quickly as possible. If the witness comes to the office by request or because he is taken there, it is usually not his choice, and this situation must not be taken advantage of. It is usually desirable to interview witnesses by arranging for an appointment at a designated time and place. If an interview of an employee at work is involved, arrange for his employer to introduce him and instruct him to cooperate with you in every way.

You must exert every effort not to incite the creation of false rumors, suspicions, or character defamation. If an identified investigator makes inquiries of friends, neighbors, employers, etc., concerning an individual, and does not reveal a reason for the activity, he will cause speculation and suspicion which frequently result in unjustified and irreparable harm to the subject of the investigation. Whenever obvious inquiries or interviews are conducted, an investigator should reveal sufficient details of the case, give satisfactory reasons for the inquiries, or substitute an appropriate pretext to prevent unwarranted speculation. It should be kept in mind that even the recognized presence of an investigator at an individual's home or office may cause speculation and might warrant covering the visit by making an appropriate explanation, or having a discussion with any curious people in the vicinity, using a pretext as an excuse for your activity.

Be alert for witnesses who are publicity seekers, and be cautious of the witness who insists on telling everything he knows. Always try to ascertain the incentives that are causing the witness to give information. Look for ulterior personal motives and abnormal mentalities. If any such unnatural situation is suspected, you should specifically check on the background, behavior, attitudes, and mental normality (as opposed to mental abnormality) of the witness before evaluating his testimony.

You must be careful so as to assure that the information came from the witness and was not suggested by yourself. Listen to all that a witness has to say about a matter, and do not discourage or ignore favorable information. Ascertain the interest and point of view of the witness to help evaluate his statements.

You should keep in mind that potentially friendly and cooperative witnesses still may not give desired information because:

1. They have faulty perception.

2. They do not remember.

3. They do not completely understand what is wanted.

4. They are not aware that they possess worthwhile information.

5. They are reluctant to get involved.

6. They are reluctant to involve others.

7. They are not impressed with the importance of cooperation.

8. They do not feel friendly toward the investigator or his agency.

9. They have been threatened or are fearful.

10. They dislike possible inconvenience or appearing in court.

11. The time or place may interfere.

12. They are unknowingly prejudiced.

13. Their logic or conclusions are faulty.

14. They mistake inferences for facts.

15. They are mentally abnormal.

B. INQUIRIES

Investigation inquiries usually represent requests for information from uninvolved and disinterested persons. Frequently, they are made casually and indifferently. Usually, the information can be had by merely asking for it and/or identifying yourself. These sources often will yield a great deal of usable evidence. Inquiries are so easy to make that you should make them early in order to take advantage of information gained when you later handle more difficult investigative activities.

Inquiries made of custodians of records that are open to the public or to recognized investigators are usually productive. For example:

1. Criminal arrest records

2. Traffic records

3. Court records

4. Real estate records

5. Post Office change-of-address cards, etc.

6. Listed telephone numbers that have been changed, and unlisted numbers

7. Birth, death, and marriage records

8. The employment records of most organizations

9. Credit rating data

10. Many others

Another type of inquiry that assists other investigation is the commonplace request for confirmation, etc., such as:

1. Asking neighbors where a certain person lives

2. Asking the postman if an individual lives at a designated address

3. Asking a child playing in the front yard if his father is home

Inquiries involving restricted information can usually be obtained by a showing of the investigator's credentials. In some cases, it may be necessary to explain in general terms why the information is necessary, or what it is to be used for. Usually, such inquiries can be made of officials or organizations without undue concern that your confidence will be betrayed.

Inquiries made of neighbors, the general public, etc., should be made carefully, using an appropriate pretext. If identity is to be revealed, it is generally desirable to ascertain the reliability and noninvolvement of the person queried.

As a rule, the first, second, or even the third inquiry of a particular source should be made in person. Thereafter, once identity and rapport have been established, the investigator may wish to make inquiries by use of the telephone, telegram, or by letter to speed the investigation and for cost reduction; however, the most complete data, etc., are usually developed through a personal, face-to-face inquiry.

C. ORIENT THE WITNESS

Before you attempt to solicit information from a witness, be sure he knows exactly what you want prior to asking questions. You should specifically designate the person or occurrence you wish to discuss. Be sure he clearly understands that you desire information about the "John Martin" who lives next door, and not the "John Martin" who works in the tool room at the plant. Frequently, identifying the person or matter to be discussed is still too general.

The witness may know enough about the designated "John Martin" to talk for several days. You may only be interested in "Martin's" hidden assets. Therefore, limit the interview to the specific topics on which you desire information.

Impress on the witness his responsibility to relate only the facts as personally known to him. Get him to agree that both the investigator and he (the witness) are interested only in the provable truth.

D. EXPLORE THE "UNKNOWN DETAILS"

The procedure for determining and listing the "unknown details" was previously discussed in Chapter 3. As a general rule, you should start an interview by asking the witness to tell (in a free-narrative discussion) what he knows about the matter being investigated, or about certain specific "unknown details." This should develop his general knowledge and may bring out unanticipated areas of knowledge. Frequently, this free-narrative discussion will resolve or sufficiently answer many of the "unknown detail" questions on your list.

All "unknown detail" questions on your list that have not been satisfactorily covered by the free-narrative discussion should be explored by direct examination. Each "unknown" should be taken separately and completed before proceeding to the next.

To explore an "unknown detail," it will generally be necessary to use a sequence of questions and answers. The sequences should proceed from general to specific, and the individual questions should be precise and discerning. Remember, a question not asked will not usually be answered, and a failure to ask the key questions is often the only reason for not resolving the "unknown." If you ask unimportant questions, you will spend your time gathering unimportant information. Usually, you cannot be sure that any issue has been completely covered during the narrative unless you re-cover the area during direct examination.

E. CROSS-EXAMINATION

Cross-examination of a witness generally should not be used when dealing with a friendly witness, but there will be times when it is necessary to test the completeness or accuracy of his testimony, and mild cross-examination may be useful.

Let the witness save face by qualifying the embarrassing answers. For example, if you were interviewing John Smith about the location and present whereabouts of John Doe and you knew that Smith saw Doe at a hotel while Smith was engaging in an extramarital affair with his secretary, you would have to alleviate Smith's fears and overcome his embarrassment. You might do so by stating: "What you do in your personal life is your total concern; I am not interested in inquiring into the circumstances surrounding your running into Doe. In fact, if these circumstances are embarrassing to you, no reference whatsoever need be made to them."

Try to separate lies from mistakes. Avoid merely trying to get the witness to confirm the information of a previous witness unless you are absolutely positive that all information given by the prior witness is factual.

Be patient with the witness whose statements are distorted, misleading, or vague. Often, the witness will believe he is doing his best to be helpful. Tactful questioning and utilization of a friendly attitude will enable you to determine the extent of a witness' knowledge and develop detailed information from him. Nervous tension may cause a witness to forget information. Try to make friendly witnesses feel at ease and confident. Even witnesses with a lower intelligence or impaired mentality can often give helpful information. Every effort should be made to test or confirm information from questionable witnesses. If a highly potential witness claims no knowledge, ask him a large number of questions concerning the matter and other topics that might in any way be associated. He will often unintentionally reveal the information you are seeking. Do not rely on the judgment of a witness concerning the relative value of any information in an investigation.

If a dying witness is interviewed, it is essential to determine if he knows or believes himself to be dying, in order to make his dying declaration admissible in court.

The applicable rule for controlling any witness is: "Gain control of the interview at the very beginning, and try to maintain that control throughout." If you lose it, take immediate steps to re-establish it, and do so in a friendly but positive manner, trying to keep the witness continuously aware that you are in control.

Preferably, do not have a pencil and paper in hand, or take notes, or take any type of statement until after a witness has had an opportunity to tell his story. However, a literal written record should *always* be made of false statements and denials of knowledge, as well as of favorable testimony, to assure proper documentation of facts and to control witnesses at a later time. A looseleaf notebook used for note-taking implies additions or deletions, so don't use one.

At the close of the interview, develop from the witness investigative leads or information of value from the casual remarks usually made by a witness.

Leave the door open for subsequent interviews, if necessary. When the interview is completed, end it. Move quickly to your next lead.

F. DETECT AND EXPLORE CLUES
OF ADDITIONAL INFORMATION

During almost every interview, there will be indicators that the witness has information which he is not revealing. Sometimes, he may be unaware of this, but often the information is intentionally concealed, restricted, or distorted because it means something unpleasant to the witness. In some cases, he may be trying to protect himself or a friend.

It is important that you detect signs of withheld information and fully explore the associated matter. Some of the clues available to the interviewer that indicate a witness has more information are:

1. Attempts to evade any question.

2. Vague answers.

3. Conflicting information.

4. Physical actions and appearance of witness.

5. Information from other sources indicating he has certain knowledge.

6. Circumstances placing him in a position to know certain information.

7. *Inconsistencies:* He knows some things; therefore, he should know others that happened at the same time.

When the withholding of information is suspected, reframe the questions and continue to explore until you get precise and discerning answers on every point in doubt.

G. TEST ASSERTIONS

Before completion of an interview, it is essential that you have detected falsehoods and separate fact from opinion. Do not accept unproven inferences as fact.

One procedure for checking the accuracy of fact is first to obtain the facts and, thereafter, check-out as many of the small details as possible. To test the assertions of a witness, you should ascertain and evaluate the conditions under which the information was obtained:

1. Determine *how* the information was obtained. If acquired by eyesight, what was the condition of the light? What distance was involved? How reliable is the eyesight of the witness? Similar questions should be considered when other senses or bodily functions are involved. If the information was related to the witness by someone else, how did the third party come by it? How reliable is the word of the third party, and what were the circumstances under which he related it? That is, was he possibly joking or gossiping? If the information was deduced from circumstances, what facts were the deductions based upon?

2. Evaluate the reliability of the witness. What is his reputation for accuracy and truthfulness? If he has been inaccurate or untruthful on one point, he may also be the same on others. How observant is

he? How good is his memory? Is he mentally competent? Does he have any personal interest in the matter?

3. Separate facts from opinions by checking and evaluating the source of the information. How did the witness get the knowledge, and how conclusive is the proof on which he bases his assertions?

Ascertain the degree of contact a witness has had with other witnesses, suspects, and occurrences in order to judge the amount of influence such contacts may have had in coloring his testimony. Get stories from all alibi witnesses and attempt to ascertain discrepancies.

Beware of the witness who lies from habit. He will usually be motivated by a desire to impress and build self-importance. He will be frequently recognized by a tendency to brag about himself, exaggerate accomplishments and abilities, and continually make assertions about the difficulties he has.

It may be necessary to use cross-examination to test or evaluate statements made by this type of witness.

Because human testimony is so variable, we do not feel that it is redundant for us to say that no matter what the testimony, always play "The Devils Advocate" and test the reliability, accuracy, and validity of all facts or assertions.

H. SUMMARIZE AND VERIFY THE TESTIMONY

After you have finished with the various phases of the interview, you should recheck to see that all of the "unknown detail" questions on your list have been satisfactorily explored, that all clues of additional information have been exploited, and that the reliability of the information has been tested.

Next, you should mentally re-arrange the information obtained so that the details follow one another in a logical continuity. Then, summarize the testimony by stating all important details in proper sequence. Stop after each statement or segment of the summary, and ask the witness to verify the correctness of your interpretation. If he indicates any disagreement, the discrepancy should be corrected before you preceed.

If the statement is to be recorded, it should be made immediately after the testimony has been summarized and verified. During the summarizing and verifying process, it is worthwhile to point out specifically the important facts and suggest that the witness

make every effort to remember them accurately, in case he is later
called on to testify in court.

I. DRAW INFERENCES AND CONCLUSIONS FROM THE INTERVIEW RESULTS

The results of an interview have little value unless they help
resolve your principal investigative objectives. First of all, they
must be relevant and material. If the testimony is to be used in
court, the facts must be admissible under the rules of evidence.

The time to evaluate these factors is at the close of the
interview, but before the witness has departed, so that any
unnecessary discrepencies can be corrected promptly. The remaining recognized discrepencies in the testimony should be kept in
mind for later attempts to corroborate by evidence from other
sources.

Much of the difficulty of drawing conclusions and evaluating
evidence comes from a failure to get all available facts together
prior to making a decision. Do not draw your conclusions until
you have completed the interview. Be careful not to base your
reasoning on false assumptions. In your initial consideration, be
skeptical of so-called facts until satisfied with the proof of their
authenticity.

Even after you are satisfied with the facts, you must use care in
interpreting them. Your conclusions will depend on the meaning
you attach to each fact. For example, a forged signature written in
a backhand style may have been written by a lefthanded suspect,
or it might have been written by some other person attempting to
disguise his writing. The alternative you choose may greatly affect
the results of your investigation.

J. HANDLING UNFRIENDLY WITNESSES

Hostile witnesses may have hidden fears that perpetuate their
hostility. This undesirable motivation may exist for many reasons,
but the following appear to be the most common:

1. They are reluctant to get involved.

2. They are reluctant to involve others.

3. They are not impressed with the importance of cooperation.

4. They are unfriendly toward the interviewer or his agency.

5. They have been threatened.

6. They dislike the inconvenience of appearing in court.

7. They are mentally abnormal.

8. They may be co-conspirators or involved in other undetected crime.

The procedure for handling hostile witnesses is somewhat contrary to that used when handling cooperative witnesses. They never volunteer information of value and frequently become uncommunicative unless properly stimulated to talk.

Begin a questioning period by discussing and asking for unobjectionable background information. Do not ask questions directly related to matter under investigation until it appears the subject will respond to such questions. Start off with easy questions that may be readily answered.

Ask for cooperation. Use leading questions that are positive in nature and convey the impression that there is no doubt of the witness' desire to cooperate; capture and retain control of subject's "submission," such as:

1. "You wish the truth to be known in this matter, do you not?"

2. "If you have any knowledge, you would naturally desire to help in procuring justice in this matter, wouldn't you?"

3. "Then I'm sure you have no objection to discussing this matter with me for a while, do you?"

Persuade him that he would expect others to help him if he were in trouble; therefore, he should assist in solving this matter that affects other citizens like himself.

Motivate him to give information. Ask him what he would conclude if a person refused to talk about a matter; imply that another person may also conclude that he could be implicated in the matter. Have a friend, an employer, a relative or an attorney advise and request him to cooperate.

Do not incite or encourage a self-secure feeling.

The witness, friendly or hostile, must always be allowed to

"save face" by qualifying all embarrassing answers. Ignore his past conduct and quietly proceed to establish rapport.

Have available a good argument and reason for overcoming excuses, such as:

1. Civic responsibility.

2. Forestalling a more serious offense, etc.

3. The rational implication that he may be involved or associated with the crime.

4. Compounding a felony.

Sometimes, exaggerating facts or stating information out of context will compel a subject to deny allegation and give correct wording. (For example: "Why did you take twice as much as your share of the money?" or "You told a falsehood when you said the money wasn't stolen, when you knew it had been removed from the locked safe.")

During the questioning, if there are indications that the subject is unwilling to talk, the conversation should immediately be changed to topics about which he spoke freely. Then, progress slowly to the desired topic via a different line of questioning.

It is frequently desirable to have a second investigator present or to make a surreptitious recording of the interview with an unfriendly witness, in case he later denies or changes his information.

In many cases, if the true reason for a witness' being hostile can be determined, it is possible to change his attitude by rationalization and persuasion. In some cases, it may be desirable to have an unfriendly witness subpoenaed by a court or other jurisdiction with the power to compel testimony under oath.

If the witness is quarrelsome, let him talk and get any grievances off his chest. After he has finished, he will usually calm down and listen to reason.

K. PRE-EMPLOYMENT INTERVIEWING

Following is a quotation from *Recruiting and Selecting Personnel*, by Arthur R. Pell: [1]

---

[1]"The Screening Interview," *Recruiting and Selecting Personnel*, (New York: Simon and Shuster, © 1969), p. 102.

The most widely used screening device for hiring all types of personnel is the screening interview. This interview may be highly effective or a complete waste of time depending on its use and the skill of the interviewer.

Interviews are conducted by employment specialists, department heads, line management, corporate executives and anyone else who can get into the act. Because most persons conducting interviews are untrained in this art, much of the employment interviewing is no more effective than a casual conversation.

For an interview to become a true screening device, the interviewer must learn how to use his technique effectively and intelligently. An interview has four major purposes:

1. to get information
2. to evaluate the applicant
3. to give information
4. to make a friend

The average applicant has many fears. The most important is the falsification of the application—usually regarding tenure of previous employment and or status levels. They also lie about their name, age, birth place, citizenship, income level, financial position, education, reason for leaving previous employments, and many other items.

Another major fear is that of the job itself. Insecurity due to fear of failure in handling the demands of the job is what this boils down to.

The next area of fear is that of the unknown. Applicants have a fear of the future, respect for seniority in lay-offs, and basic employee treatment. These are all unknowns and prey on the applicant's mental process.

As a result of these fears, he will form attitudes that are defensive. He will attempt to deceive the interviewer by attempting to make a good impression. He will dress, act, and talk the way he believes he should to get the job. He will hide what he feels to be detrimental to his obtaining the job. Note: All of this is his concept and may be vastly different from the objectives of the interview, which are to ascertain the applicant's qualifications for the job and to fit him to the job specifications. The fitting of "square pegs into round holes" is what we are trying to avoid, and the problem is that the average applicant, because of fear, projects a varying image that at one moment is round and another moment, square.

He may upgrade his qualifications, or even downgrade them, in order to obtain employment.

From the authors' experience, the objectives in interviewing job applicants at rank-and-file level are:

1. Ascertain if the applicant has the necessary skills to meet the job specifications or job description.

2. Will the applicant's personality blend with the specified job he is being interviewed for?

3. Are there any abnormalities (physio-psycho) that would interfere with his filling a specified job?

4. Is there a history of abnormality (physio-psycho) that might indicate a trend toward disqualifying the applicant from the specified job?

5. Does the applicant possess the necessary potential that would lead beyond the specified job?

6. Can the applicant meet other specifications set by management for the individual company and job, such as, medical and security.

7. Does the applicant have the character or integrity to meet management's standards? A cardinal rule in personnel interviewing is that during the interview, one does not interrogate; in other words, the technique of cross-examination is not used in a pre-employment screening interview. On the other hand, all too frequently we have seen personnel interviewers ask: "You have not been arrested, have you?" Is not this interviewer asking for a "No" answer?

The management applicant is subject to exactly the same fears as the "low man on the totem pole." However, because of the weight of the position in the industrial scale, the pressures are considerably greater. The management applicant is concerned with job potential and advancement. He is also more likely to attempt deception concerning his previous salary, rather than tenure. He can be expected to be even more solicitous to the interviewer. He will perform as an actor much more than the average, rank-and-file applicant. Most of this is due to his having been schooled to know what image he is expected to present to get the job.

The objectives of the management applicant interviewer are identical with those stated earlier, with this additional point: Because management must recommend, make and help make decisions, rather than perform tasks of production skill, the investigator/interviewer must be able to determine whether the applicant will perform well and make or implement decisions *under pressure.*

L. PRE-PROMOTIONAL AND TRANSFER INTERVIEWING

Pre-promotional and transfer interviewing is specialized, and the subject's fears are specific at any job level:

1. Whom do I have to cut down to get the promotion or the transfer?

2. Who is going to try to cut me down?

3. Are they paying me enough to want the promotion or transfer?

4. What long-range opportunities will this promotion or transfer induce?

The objectives of pre-promotional and transfer interviewing can be confined to a few areas:

1. Is the employee physically suitable for the promotion or transfer?

2. Does the employee have the emotional stability deemed necessary for the promotion or transfer?

3. Is the employee adequately equipped by background, training, character, integrity, and experience for the promotion or transfer?

4. Has the employee's maturity level developed to the point where he will be loyal to the purposes of the promotion or transfer?

5. Can we develop from the employee a clear picture of all problems at the job level being vacated, so that manage-

ment may be totally informed and be positioned to make necessary changes?

M. SYSTEMS AND OPERATIONAL INTERVIEWING

These areas are chamelion-like, in that they sometimes assume the color and proportions of a quasi-criminal interrogation. Accompanying any system is a written approach which provides guidelines and standards that can be administered and audited; however, people are imperfect, and the sytem always breaks down. The attempt to ascertain the level of responsibility for a system or to correct systematic weakness can produce considerable pressure on both the interviewer and the interviewee.

Responsibility for a system breakdown is usually accompanied by mild to extreme underlying guilt feelings, even though the interviewee is in no way responsible. Nevertheless, this creates fear in that type of interviewing. When the interviewer is looking for weaknesses in the system it is normal for the interviewee to have guilt feelings which may cause him to believe erroneously that the objective of the discussion is to fix responsibility on him for malfunctions. This can lead to the interviewee attempting deception.

If the interviewer does not wish to induce guilt, he should advise the interviewee that the purpose is not to fix responsibility. The objectives of systems and operations interviewing are to identify and develop the systematic weakness present or to correct the operational breakdown. Since the objectives of this type of interviewing have been shown to be the cause of guilt and fear in the interviewee, it may be necessary to conceal the true purpose of the interview.

The subterfuge for such interviewing should blend with the parent situation. For example: Tell the interviewee that he is closer to the given area than anyone else, and that his assistance will help broaden management's over-view and understanding. Once the general area to be explored is reached and the interviewee is convinced that he is a "full partner" in the inquiry, then, in very general terms alluding to the weakness or breakdown, ask: "How would you handle it, and what recommendation would you make?" Never directly ask the interviewee a question about a system that would fix responsibility for the breakdown on him.

Many of those interviewed concerning system and operations breakdowns will voluntarily accept responsibility in order to gain your sympathy. This responsibility should be rationalized away so as not to confuse the true issues.

N. INTERVIEWING WOMEN

1. We note that when women are interviewed by an interviewer of either sex, they tend to respond more emotionally than men. They may react with greater emotion than most men although the end product could be identical.

2. As a result of the dual standard in our society, women tend to be more defensive in male/female competitive situations. Because of the dual standard, some women may use "the white lie" as a defense—still, a lie by our definition may mislead the interviewer.

3. As a general statement, it has been noted that people who confront guilt emotionally respond in an altogether different way than those who cope with guilt intellectually. May we point out that most women will tend to respond emotionally by training (as most men will respond intellectually through training). The emotional dissipation of guilt offers greater temporary relief than suppression of the feeling and intellectual rationalization of it.

To interview women effectively, it may be necessary for the interviewer to be more receptive to emotional content. Since women frequently communicate at more personal, subjective levels than men, a greater degree of understanding may be required by the objectively oriented interviewer. Any attempt on the part of the interviewer to inhibit the flow of subjective content, especially if strong emotions or feelings are involved, will usually result in an almost immediate breakdown of rapport.

8

HOW TO INTERROGATE

8

HOW TO INTERROGATE

A. WHY DO SUSPECTS CONFESS?

Suspects make admissions or confessions because they are in a state of mind which leads them to believe cooperation is the best course of action to follow. There may be many personal reasons inhibiting the development of such a state of mind, but the effective use of proper interviewing/interrogation techniques will usually result in overcoming these inhibitions.

As a rule, suspects committed their crimes in the belief that such conduct offered the best solution to their needs at the moment. Often, it is difficult for us to comprehend why an individual commits an act that quite obviously may result in severe punishment or other undesirable retribution. Why does the suspect confess, knowing the probable consequences? Actions that are investigated are found to be motivated. The fact that they do not appear to be in the subject's self-interest does not contradict the fact that the act was motivated. Most criminal acts eventually prove detrimental to the welfare of the perpetrator. Usually, violators who have previous criminal records are aware of the probable consequences.

Inability to understand the motivation for a particualr crime is due to the interrogator's inability to comprehend the fears, inferiority complexes, passions, morals, physical drives, mental abnormalities, attitudes, ambitions, environmental pressures, and other complex forces which are very real and compelling to one individual, but may seem trivial or unimportant to others. These same complex forces are acting upon the perpetrator while he is being interrogated, and a working knowledge of those interfering inhibitions or potential incentives to cooperate is advantageous. However, armed with this essential knowledge, more powerful psychological and physiological factors may be employed to influence the violator's state of mind, leading to admissions or confessions.

During our discussion of the physical and the psychological influences appearing in Chapters 5 and 6, we noted that the body and brain function as a coordinate unit and that many physical variables were present during the interview/interrogation. We specifically pointed to the emotions of anger, fear, and neutral excitement. We have shown the physical symptoms of emotion, now let us present the concept that these physical and mental variables may be assembled into a logical sequence which, in turn, will produce that influence which alters the violator's state of mind.

B. PRE-INTERROGATION CONSIDERATIONS

To interrogate is to examine formally and officially by the use of questioning and persuasion for the purpose of inducing a person to reveal intentionally concealed information. The information developed may be, and usually is, self-incriminating in nature.

It is easy to feel resentment toward a suspect because he resists, but you should bear in mind that it is natural for him to do so. His future welfare is at stake; and, in most cases, he would not have committed the act if he felt certain that he would be discovered. If you look at the situation through his eyes, you must conclude that it is completely normal for him to offer many forms of resistance.

Learn to expect resistance from perpetrators and to develop an understanding attitude, and learn to allow your very being to be challenged to the degree necessary to overcome. In fact, if you give the outward impression that you expect a suspect to resist, and indicate respect for his viewpoint, you may well establish yourself as a friendly opponent in the struggle to win, rather than an enemy. Look upon the interrogation as a great game, and upon winning or losing as not being important.

Resistance may take the forms of refusal to talk, failure to cooperate, the use of alibis, strong protests of innocence, lies, attempts to flee, arrogance, etc. The types of resistance used by an individual can reveal much about the nature of his character and thinking, and indicate the specific countermeasures to be taken.

Never allow yourself to be put on the defensive. In many cases, some forms of resistance can be prevented by anticipating a suspect's reactions and countering them with appropriate arguments or explanations before they arise. This places you on the *offensive,* and you must always be "in the driver's seat."

Interrogators frequently reason in terms of their own feelings, instead of those of the suspect. Conclusions drawn from such thinking are subject to greater error than if the interrogators try to see, hear, feel, and think from the suspect's viewpoint.

Success in influencing a suspect is dependent upon the elimination or overcoming of his resistance to cooperation. Suggestion is more effective than argument; reasoning is more effective than demanding. Analyze, and counter each resistance factor by the most effective means possible.

Most mental and physical functions of the body are affected by outside influences, and the degree of the effect will depend upon the strength of the influence. In general, a strong influence will produce a strong reaction and a weak influence, a weak reaction. Of equal significance, a strong effect can be produced by an accumulation of small influences. In operation, these principles mean:

1. A suspect may be induced to confess because of a strong influence, such as proof of his fingerprints on a weapon.

2. He may confess because of the cumulative influence of a number of small persuasions, no one of which is sufficient to produce the desired effect.

   For example, the combined influence of proof-of-motive, proof-of-opportunity, removal of fear of confederates, development of remorse, and elimination of false impressions about probable extent of punishment may motivate a violator to confess; but no one (or several) of these factors would be sufficient to induce the confession.

In cases where we have strong pressures to use during interrogation, we usually have no difficulty in getting admissions; however, when no strong pressure is available, we are faced with a totally different set of influence factors. In such instances, we must reduce all resistance factors and stimulate all the incentives to confess. No factor is too small to receive attention. A small influence may be comparable to "the straw that broke the camel's back."

There is also a lot of truth in another old adage which says, "Seeing is believing." People are more inclined to believe what they sense directly than what is told them. A suspect will be more convinced of something he sees, smells, feels, or tastes than of something he is told. It is profitable to take advantage of every opportunity to use aids or auxiliaries as referred to in Chapter 3.

It is important to be alert to "yes" signs that the suspect is willing to make admissions or a confession. The proper psychological moment to stimulate such utterances may occur at any time. The information may be volunteered or may require the application of strong influences before the right moment to solicit it is reached. *Casual inquiries* made while the violator is still under the emotional shock of the crime are often productive. The resistance of the violator may also be low at the time of apprehension and other similar periods when his fear and anxiety are strong enough to paralyze temporarily his reasoning ability. As a general rule, *the ability to reason decreases as the emotions increase.*

Adjust your questioning speed to the mental limitations of both yourself and the suspect. If you are interrupted at any time during the interview, it is usually desirable to review the points made prior to the break.

Frequently, a suspect will be less fortified if interviewed by surprise.

It is always desirable to advise suspects immediately of their constitutional rights. If the procedure of informing the individual of his rights is performed in a friendly and consoling manner at the very outset, it will usually convince the suspect of the investigator's integrity and set the stage for the suspect to make admissions later. Moreover, that procedure removes the threat of the confession's being inadmissible later in any proceeding.

Make suspects comfortable, but do not coddle them. *Establish a friendly atmosphere, but never let the suspect develop any doubt about your competence and your complete control of the interrogation.* Seat suspects in a comfortable but plain chair where the entire body action can be observed. The chair should be placed with the back toward the door of the room, to minimize the distraction of anyone entering or leaving the room. The location of the interview/interrogation was discussed in Chapter 3.

Frequently, it is possible to get worthwhile background information directly from a suspect prior to questioning him about the matter under investigation. If a suspect's office, home, or person has been lawfully searched, etc., make an examination of the fruits of the crime—writing on scraps of paper or matchbooks, transportation ticket stubs, receipts, clothing labels, club membership cards, and any unusual items may give clues to be explored during the questioning.

After all background information has been examined, the interrogator should attempt to estimate the degree and kind of information one might expect the suspect to possess. With this evaluation in mind, you are in a position to recognize deviations and immediately explore unsuspected ramifications or discount information which is obviously false.

C. UNDERMINE SUSPECT'S CONFIDENCE OF SUCCESS

As long as a perpetrator feels he can escape detection or punishment, he will not be receptive to persuasion that he should cooperate. He will not surrender himself psychologically as long as he feels successful, any more than a general who believes that he is winning a battle will surrender his army. While this psychological state of mind exists, he will not consider furnishing any incriminating data. *You must undermine his confidence in escaping* before he will be receptive to any alternative solution. Essentially, this process consists of blocking all noncooperative avenues of escape. It involves detecting his lies, discrediting his alibis, preventing physical flight, emphasizing the quality and quantity of incriminating evidence and other information derogatory to the subject.

We have noted certain signals which indicate a criminal violator is confident of escape. These are:

1. Arrogance

2. Unresponsiveness to suggestions of cooperation.

In Chapter 3, the authors commented on location of the interview. Further, the location selected for the interrogation should not have the appearance of a detention cell, but it should have characteristics that will convince the suspect that there is little chance for physical flight.

After rapport has been established, you should initiate the interrogation by soliciting the most complete *free-narrative* account of the crime or related incidents of which the suspect may have knowledge. Up to this point, you should neither contradict nor show any signs of skepticism. Let the suspect lie and distort information if he desires. If you are sure he has made a number of incorrect statements that can be proven false, it may be desirable to take a written statement from him incorporating the falsehoods. When you later prove the falsity of any of the facts, point out how detrimental the statement is to the suspect, and offer to be a friend by permitting him to substitute a correct statement or amendments to the original. Thus, you undermine his confidence, as well as create a strong incentive for him to confess.

Analyze the testimony for clues which indicate deception, omissions, or distortions, and use cross-examination to explore these areas further. You may raise points for further clarification or discrediting the subject. Incorporate any gains, and do not attempt to explore or develop any areas that will cause conflicts, for it is generally advantageous to refrain from pointing out conflicts and lies *when* they occur. If you call attention to discrepancies as they appear, you will allow for the suspect to make individual explanations and adjust his story to conform to the explanation, thereby setting his defenses against any further slips. When he is confronted with a number of discrepancies at any one time, his excuses or protests are ineffective and his confidence is usually greatly reduced. Advise the subject of the discrepancies in a continuous sequence (Bang! Bang! Bang!), emphasizing the seriousness of each and allowing the subject little or no time to protest or explain.

During this phase of interrogation, the use of free narrative, direct examination, and cross-examination should be specifically designed to trap the suspect verbally and to demonstrate the futility of his position. Sometimes you may stage a situation as an effective means of undermining confidence. These staged situations may be useful when the suspect insists that he knows nothing about the crime. Never bluff if there is the least chance that the suspect will detect the bluff.

A suspect is usually more convinced by specific illustrations and physical evidence than he is by alleged statements of his guilt or by circumstantial evidence.

We note that when the suspect appears pensive and submissive, he is probably losing his confidence (of escape in any form) and is ready for a discussion of the alternatives. In some cases, it will be necessary to resume the process of undermining confidence from time to time throughout the remainder of the interrogation in order to keep him in a receptive mood to submissive cooperation.

D. OFFER THE SUSPECT A MUTUALLY ACCEPTABLE SOLUTION

Offer the suspect a solution to the basis for his interrogation that allows for cooperation and which can be made to appear *less objectionable* to him than other courses of action that he might follow. *Make your solution appear attractive by emphasizing the disadvantages or negative qualities of any other possible solution.* Try to convince the suspect that:

1. He is confronted with a personal emergency.

2. Since he cannot escape, he must find a way out.

3. No available solution will be pleasant.

4. Your proposal should result in less unpleasantness than any of the other solutions.

Your proposals and justifications must be designed to suit each individual and each act. Relate the alternatives to the suspect's wants and needs, and point out the bad points of other solutions in relation to his fears and aversions. Convince him that your suggested solution is the best one to meet his needs in the current emergency. More concerning this will be developed in Chapter 9.

E. MAKE SUBMISSION TOLERABLE

Gain the confidence and respect of the suspect. When a person desires to confide his troubles voluntarily, he does not go to an enemy or confederate, but rather to a parent, clergyman, medical doctor, lawyer, close friend, or some other respected person who he feels will understand, console, and advise him. When a criminal violator confesses, he, in reality, surrenders his very being and his own free will and destiny into the hands of the interrogator, etc. He will find it much easier to submit if he believes in the interrogator's integrity and is sympathetic to his position He must believe that the interrogator is neither prosecutor, judge, nor jury.

The behavior of the interrogator must be superior to that of the suspect during the interrogation. Be friendly, exhibit interest, but avoid fraternizing with him. It is also important to avoid appearing superior in a way that would make the suspect appear to be stupid. Be tactful and considerate of his feelings. Most people desire understanding and consideration at the time when they deserve it the least. When a suspect can give reasons for cooperating, he can satisfy his own conscience and save face with others. Any procedure which will permit the criminal violator to "save face" or retain his pride may be effective in fostering the initial breakthrough. "Breakthrough" will be further discussed in Chapter 10.

F. ENCOURAGE ACQUIESCENCE AND PURSUE INDICATORS OF COMPLIANCE

When it appears that the suspect's confidence of escape has been shaken and he appears interested in your suggestions, you should begin to diminish other confession-inhibiting factors and promote incentives to confess. Discount his fears, accentuate futility of further resistance, sympathize, exploit appropriate emotions and attitudes, and other influencing techniques.

Clues to the subject's attitudes and character may be deduced by carefully observing him during the preliminary interrogation, as well as by asking specific questions and analyzing the answers for hidden indications of personal feelings.

A procedural approach for reducing confession-inhibiting factors which involves the rational countering of fears, doubts, and apprehensions may be developed in the following steps:

1. A strong *fear of punishment* may be indicated by the suspect's inquiries as to what kind of punishment or what penitentiaries offenders are generally sent to, the subject's interest in making bond, and jail time.

To counter the fear of punishment, point out to the suspect that jail time may be much less than he anticipates. If appropriate, you could advise your subject of the probation procedures, light fines, and that short sentences are frequently given in similar cases.

Extreme care should be taken so as not to promise or give the impression that you will arrange for him light punishment, etc., if he confesses.

2. *Fear of the effect that his involvement may have on his family, friends and employer* may be indicated by inquires of the existence of a family, friend(s), and an employer. Susceptibility to this fear may be deduced from his past record of reputable conduct and faithfulness to such associates. Ascertain if the character of his family, friends, or employer are such that they would probably be shocked by knowledge of the suspect's criminal violation.

To reduce his concern about his family, friends, and employer, impress on him that, regardless of what he has done, his family and employer will be more forgiving to a person who has confessed his error and cooperated in every way to right the wrong.

3. The interrogator must also be particularly aware that some criminal violators have, as an underlying motive, the need for punishment. Karpman[1] speaks of "guilt drives," wherein the offender subconsciously leaves clues in an unconscious effort to be caught and punished.

Those who appear to be compelled psychologically toward punishment must be identified by the interrogator so that he will not rationalize away this very strong motivation for cooperation. The most common signals of this self-destructive type of personality are statements literally requesting punishments.

We have noted that this type of personality is best dealt with by not rationalizing any fears and not amplifying these fears.

---

[1]Karpman, Benjamin, *The Sex Offender and His Offenses*, Julian Press, 1954.

4. *Any concern that the subject may have about the welfare or opinion of co-conspirators* is usually diminished by condemning the co-conspirators and blaming them for the suspect's predicament. Limit your interrogation to developing all information about the crime, and advise the suspect that he need not name the co-conspirators. Usually, the suspect will later name the co-conspirators himself, following the "yes" attitude created by furnishing the initial information.

5. *If the suspect is fearful of being called a "squealer,"* try to convince him that admitting his part in the crime is not squealing. Impress on him that the co-conspirators will not hesitate to "tell all" the facts concerning the crime and lay all the blame on him.

6. There may be signs of *apprehension about future employment.* If appropriate, try to convince the suspect that his present employer usually takes a sympathetic view following a statement of truth and may not look too seriously on his troubles if he (the subject) does everything possible to avoid publicity and clear up the trouble as quickly as possible. Try to impress upon the subject that if he cooperates and clears up the current matter, there are always many other places of employment which may not require a background investigation.

7. *Fear of retaliation to one's-self or family by co-conspirators* may be created by information suggesting the ruthless nature of his associates or knowledge that threats have been made. The suspect may exhibit concern that his associates had observed his arrest or seen him in the company of an investigator.

Try to convince the suspect that if he makes a full confession (statement) and cooperates completely, the co-conspirators will probably do the same or be taken into custody. We note that seldom do co-conspirators become a threat to one's personal safety; usually, this is due to their preoccupation with their own defense.

8. *Deep concern about protection of one's reputation* may be indicated by the suspect's having a respected position in the community or in his employment, and the strong probability of jeopardizing such position if his wrongdoing becomes known.

To counter this, minimize the moral seriousness of the crime. Try to convince the suspect that there would be less harm to his reputation if he admitted error and impressed everyone that the mistake would not be repeated, than if he were to remain under the "cloud" of suspicion or stand trial and be convicted.

9. *Stubbornness* is detected by an unusual persistence in adhering to jobs, rackets, hangouts, associates, statements, etc., even though evident that such action is not in his best interest. Other signs of stubbornness will be noted in the subject's refusal to face facts or admit situations which it may be proven have occurred.

Overcome stubbornness by rationalizing with the suspect, pointing out the advantages of confessing and the disadvantages of not confessing. Give plausible answers to all excuses made by the suspect.

10. *Often, violators have a strong compulsion not to surrender stolen money or property.* This situation should usually be expected to exist in cases where the original motive of the crime was to obtain money and/or property.

Try to weaken this desire by convincing the suspect that the particular money or property involved can be identified (if appropriate) and, therefore, would trap him. Also, try to convince him that law-enforcement officers will watch him indefinitely—including his family and friends—and unless he surrenders the money or property, he and his family can never feel free to live as normal citizens.

11. *Highly emotional types* of individuals may be recognized by outbursts of temper or positive identification of having committed emotional-type crimes; such as rape, assault and battery, hit and run, etc.

In addition to recognizing and repressing the confession-inhibiting factors, you should recognize and accentuate factors that will motivate the confession.

1. *Remorsefulness:* Some clues that remorsefulness exists, or can be developed in a suspect, are:

    a. Church connections.

b. Close family ties.

c. Close friendship with persons of good character.

d. The commission of emotionally motivated crimes.

e. An individual who stands to lose much of his hard-earned gains in life.

f. Signs of anguish; such as, facial contortions, wringing of hands, pacing floor, etc.

If the suspect is of reasonably strong moral character, he should be continuously impressed with his crimes and the need for him to cleanse his soul, mind, and body, and to show contrition immediately, starting to re-establish his good name and character.

Point out the impossibility of ever completely removing the gnawing distress arising from the suspect's sense of guilt for his past overt acts if he does not admit his mistake(s) and tell the truth. Remind him that he must "look at himself in the mirror" each morning and live with himself the rest of his life; if he is to have "peace of mind" for the rest of his days, he will have to rid himself of self-punishment, his own "hell." Tell the suspect that he will have the feelings of a hunted animal if he does not remove the matter from his mental processes. Point out the details of his guilty appearance; such as, the physical indicators of stress discussed in Chapter 5.

2. *The desire for sympathy* and friendship may be indicated by:

a. Lack of friends and relatives to turn to.

b. Complaints of "raw deals" and bad luck.

c. Statements that he is "being framed," "picked on," or "double-crossed."

Encourage the suspect to talk about his misfortunes and troubles. Sympathizing with him on things that are troubling him in general, you will note, will make it easier for him to talk about the matter at issue. Tell him that many others have done the same thing and have lived it down. If you can get a suspect to confide and talk about his troubles, he will often give clues to the "Why's" and begin to make admissions about the crime

3. Appeal to the suspect's *pride*. Use well-selected flattery. Make him feel that it "takes guts" to admit a wrongdoing for which he knows he may be punished. Convince him that it is cowardly to hide behind lies when he knows he cannot escape. Tell him that a real man would stand up and admit his deeds.

4. Rationalize with the suspect that evidence that points to his guilt. Point out to him that he would not draw any other conclusion from the facts if his position were reversed. If you tell him he has lied, be sure you can substantiate each and every instance to him.

Emphasize futility in giving further resistance. (Advise him not to "bang his head against a stone wall," etc.)

If the situation appears to be developing into a stalemate, a complete change of atmosphere is suggested. Relax and give the impression that you are no longer trying to convince him. You may even act as though you were ready to depart. Then, quickly make what appears to be several departing remarks about your strongest persuasion points. It may be productive to solicit his confession by indicating this is a last chance for him to help himself through cooperation. Make these maneuvers quickly— before he has a chance to raise his defenses again.

Throughout the questioning, try to frame questions and describe situations in such a way that agreeing with you is generally easier than disagreeing. The more often he agrees with you on general points, the harder it is to disagree on important points.

Most resistance encountered early in the interrogation will be excuses; but later, opposition is usually genuine. No matter how many times you try unsuccessfully to get the suspect to submit, you must keep the way open for further discussion. Regardless of what a suspect may say or do, he has not accepted your persuasion until he actually cooperates with you and furnishes provable information.

Near the end of an unsuccessful interrogation, you may consider the advisability of making concessions or liberalizing your proposal. For instance, the compulsion to retain stolen money may be inhibiting a suspect from confessing. If he is willing to admit the theft without revealing the location of the money, it may be desirable to allow the violator to confess only to the crime and temporarily retain the money, rather than to fail on both counts. Great care must be exercised in making concessions or agreements. Always have the legal and administrative right to negotiate the concession contemplated. This means, simply, to *make no promises that you cannot keep.*

G. CONSOLIDATE ACCOMPLISHMENTS

The final step in gaining admissions or confessions is the recognition of the correct psychological moment to stimulate submission. Thereafter, the process of drawing the information from the suspect, known as expansion, is in order. More about the expansion process and that psychological moment called "break-through" will be discussed in Chapter 10.

Look for signs of weakening; such as, "What do you think I'd get if I confessed?" etc. When such signs become evident, continue the persuasion process with renewed effort. *"Stay with him."*

During initial admissions, let him save face by omitting embar-rassing details. Try first to obtain admissions of less important details or minor offenses. Should the subject weaken on minor details, he will usually add more and more information under skillful interrogation, until the entire criminal act has been covered. The interrogator must obtain a clearcut admission of the criminal act.

In some cases, it may help if you can get one of his parents, his wife, a close friend, his employer, a clergyman, or his lawyer to persuade the suspect to cooperate and admit his part in the criminal act.

When the interrogator is tired and inclined to give up, he should always continue with confidence and renewed vigor. The suspect may be close to cooperating at that point, and he too may be fatigued. Under more stress by the interrogator, the "break-through" may follow.

If the subject fully submits, you can use the procedures described in Chapter 2 under "The Seven W's" to acquire the details systematically.

When a criminal violator does submit and agrees to cooperate, the gain should be immediately consolidated and rendered as irreversible as possible. This is an accomplished fact if you discuss all details of the crime with the violator, taking statements, arranging for witnesses or recordings, having him admit guilt to family or friends or other witnesses, identifying instruments of the crime, obtaining a description of the location of contraband fruits of the crime, and having the subject provide names of confederates, etc. The more he confirms his guilt, the less likely he will be to refute his admissions later.

H. INTERROGATING SUSPECTS OF QUESTIONABLE GUILT

Since the suspect's involvement is questionable, this becomes one of the rare cases where the interrogator cannot take a positive direction in his questioning; therefore, it is necessary to assume a neutral attitude. If you start by assuming either guilt or innocence, it will often lead to situations that are difficult to correct, should it later become apparent that an incorrect assumption was made.

The questioning should begin by asking the suspect if he knows the basis for the interrogation. If he says "No," you may be able to prove to him at the outset that he is lying and thus immediately undermine his resistance. In some cases, he will give early information or make admissions about violations or occurrences of which there was no previous knowledge.

Prejudging a suspect's involvement merely because of his appearance, mannerisms, reputation, or past record is unprofessional. Even a major criminal may not have committed the particular crime in which you are interested.

Use free narrative, direct examination, and cross-examination to the maximum extent in deciding the suspect's degree of implication. Ask many questions and avoid showing any reactions to his answers.

Summarize by going over the facts of the occurrence in great detail, while watching the suspect's reactions. The facts will impress and affect the composure of the involved person much more than they will an innocent person.

One method of ascertaining composure and possible involvement is the practice of applying neutral stimuli wherein the interrogator introduces a few known facts that are collateral to the act under investigation. These facts are inserted among stimuli of a relatively similar nature. The suspect is observed closely for any visible psycho/physio responses to pertinent facts.

At the end of this process, *if you are convinced* the suspect is involved, continue with cross-examining interrogation procedures. If you are positive that the suspect is innocent, apologize for any inconvenience to him. If you are still in doubt, just thank him and advise that he may possibly be recontacted.

If the suspect is involved, you will have left extreme uncertainty, which could be a favorable factor during further questioning or investigation. At the same time, an innocent person will not be too concerned, because he does not have the inherent fear of discovery that always exists with violators.

9

EMOTIONAL INROADS

9

EMOTIONAL INROADS

A. THE FATHER OR RESPECTED FIGURE IMAGE

We are aware that a well-known household detergent's trademark was designed to emulate the physical appearance of a political figure (the then president of the U.S.). This "father image" was created to break down sales resistance and inspire confidence in the product. Another example of the father image is that of the kindly, gray-haired police officer who obtains confessions with seeming ease, while the younger appearing detective experiences considerable difficulties under very similar sets of conditions.

The father image seems to inspire the subject's confidence mainly by breaking down the defensive abilities of the suspect. One might pose the question to one's-self that, as a child, have you ever tried to lie to your father or your mother? Difficult, wasn't it? This awe of the parental image and lack of defense against it lies buried within all of us, even if we have antipathy toward our fathers or mothers.

Age is not the key component for achieving the father image. We note that young men can project a father image to others who could be their grandparents. To project this image, one must possess the professional attitude that inspires confidence and respect—sympathy, understanding, firmness and, above all, the ability to fulfill the subject's own, individual picture of their father. We do not mean that the interviewer need physically look like the subject's father. What we seek is the subject's psychological concept of his father, respected parent, or other relation, etc. To obtain this concept is a matter of extremely subtle initial questioning technique about family, family relationships, and finally "the respected figure." When the subject can be brought into the position of offering a description of his "respected figure" image, then the interviewer is in a position of strength in terms of projecting such an image.

One highly successful method of obtaining the necessary information is that of the interviewer himself leading the conversation to a nostalgic area and then bringing forth the "respected figure" image. Any anecdote used need not be true and should relate somewhat to the personality of the subject. For example, were the subject a fisherman, a story about a fishing experience involving the interviewer's father could be told. Story-telling of the fishing experience should produce the necessary nostalgia to cause the subject to recite a similar type of story, which may or may not be truthful. By careful nurturing, further stories about the subject's father, or the "respected figure," can be elicited. That they are or are not the truth is of no consequence, since the subject is revealing the concept of a "respected figure" that he already possesses.

The interviewer then assembles all the important and projectable features of the subject's "respected figure" image and proceeds to assume them gradually. Mature judgment is required to know when to stop the flow of personal nostalgia and allow for the subject's counter-flow of information to come forth. This same judgment is necessary "to separate the wheat from the chaff" with regard to the projectable portions of the subject's father, or "respected figure," image concept.

Therefore, when the interviewer projects an image that matches the subject's concept of the "respected figure," the subject's defenses are reduced and deterrents to deception are established. The subject's concept of the "respected figure" image is obtainable by studying his subjective needs and conscious desires. The subject's concept, once assessed, is then assumed or projected back at him through the interviewer's acting-out process.

B. NORMAL PERSONALITY INSECURITY

1. Need for Expiation

The emotional "Achilles' heel" of the human personality is insecurity. Insecurity exists in all human personalities in varying degrees. Insecurity is the interviewer's/interrogator's strongest ally or worst enemy. Whether friend or foe, its usefulness is dependent upon the interviewer's/interrogator's use of it.

This is not the insecurity produced by the commission of overt acts. It is the normal insecurity that is neurotically instilled in all personalities living within the complex society we inhabit.

At a tender age of "X" months, the mother yells at baby in the crib. The infantile concept of this produces insecurity. The insecurity produced magnifies over the years and is fed by any situation that is of a neurotic trend. Insecurity produces anxiety, which results in the production of further insecurity. When this process exceeds certain limits, the normal person's personality becomes neurotic.

For purposes of this discussion, the neurosis is defined as a state of mind wherein the subject's psychic energies are controlled by the constant need to defend the present mental status quo. It may express itself as various complaints without apparent organic cause. The neurotic trend is an embryo neurosis, caused by conflict within the personality—usually environmentally based.

Insecurity normal to any personality is a pliant or moveable tool. Correctly adjusted and used, insecurity can produce a condition of oral catharsis that exceeds the potent intestinal effects of castor oil. Insecurity via guilt can motivate fear, defensive attitudes, and deception, if not channelled. Much of what we attempt to achieve through the removal of fear is partial control of the subject's normal insecurity feelings. Creation of rapport and establishment of the "respected figure" image gives us a direct means of exercising further control over insecurity and guilt.

Insecurity that is formed normally at the infant level usually translates into guilt feelings, because the infant is concerned only with self. The question, "What have I done to produce this treatment of me?" later becomes "I am the cause" by association, because the infant lacks the critical judgment which would have led him to say: "I may not be the cause."

The insecurity translated to guilt feelings normal to the personality leads to an inescapable need for expiation or atonement on the part of most people. Various theologies have made capital use of this need for expiation for thousands of years. The offer of salvation, with its guaranteed release from anxiety feelings for the doer of good deeds, reinforces the theological position. The theological introduction of the all-inclusive embodiment called sin, or evil, and the hell and torment awaiting those who perpetrate iniquitous acts or sins, further reinforces the normal insecurity and subsequent guilt feelings in man. In turn, this strengthens the release from anxiety when achieving expiation.

Examination of human neurosis in terms of guilt feelings shows much evidence of the related need for expiation, which surfaces as the constant striving for approval. General conformity of neurotics (sharing the guilt), the continual need to reinforce their own security, and their need to constantly prove the truth to themselves are other surface effects of the insecurity-guilt cycle. While neurotic man devotes most of his psychic energies to escape from guilt feelings, those people on the norm, search at a more modest rate. Even those well-adjusted to complex living, however, have a need to escape an undefinable guilt at any one time or another. The escape shows up as dependence on alcohol, aspirin, television, or even golf. One of the authors freely admits that his fishing trips are more for escape than for sportsmanship. Many escapes begin as the need for expiation and are later translated into a desire for fulfillment.

2. Insecurity or Guilt Feeling Amplification as a Tool

As we become aware of the need for expiation, we begin to see the use of this personality component for our own interview/ interrogation ends. Foremost in the scheme is the amplification of personal guilt feelings brought on by the earlier described insecurity. This is the process of turning the guilt which has been exhibited upon itself to magnify the anxiety of internal stress produced. There are various methods for doing this.

One of the most common methods of guilt feelings amplification is to increase insecurity of personal position. This can be done by some very simple devices. Among the more successful is the "Please repeat that" device. At a critical point in an interview, where the subject is showing very stiff defensive attitudes, the query, "Please repeat that, I'm not sure I heard you correctly," immediately forces the subject to shift his defensive focus to that point in question—to determine how he has blundered. The obvious conclusion he draws is that he has somehow psychologically betrayed his inner concepts. For the moment, he may rationalize away his defensive attitudes and reiterate the statement. The insecurity that has been created by the associative thought, that he has somehow erred, cannot be erased however. This insecurity must go somewhere and will usually turn inward to feed the guilt component smouldering within. This subtle attack on a single defensive point results in the subject's believing that there is a psycho-self-denouncement, which then allows the interviewer/ interrogator to proceed and expand his line of thought without too much opposition.

Another common method of building amplification of guilt as it relates to insecurity is to play the role of the expert. When people are confronted with what they believe is a precise and exact knowledge of any given subject, they begin to doubt that their own knowledge is sufficient and become insecure. When, during the course of an interview, the interrogator speaks with an aura of positive knowledge (not arrogance), the insecurity process the subject formerly experienced begins anew. This is the main reason that all interviewers must be positive in their commentary. Anything less than a positive positioning should be omitted from the interview. Even neutrality must be positively stated.

Sometimes the subject will attempt to seize control by asking: "Are you accusing me?" The interviewer, in preserving absolute neutrality, must state: "I don't know whether you are or are not involved." The regaining of control is accomplished by: "I am in possession of the facts that will absolve those not involved and put those involved right into it."

An excellent form of amplification of guilt is the Rogerian nondirective approach, wherein the last words of the subject are fed back to him by the interviewer. Great care must be taken when using this method, as it can also cause an almost uncontrollable release of aggression toward the operator (interviewer/interrogator). Unless the bond of rapport is quite strong, this method can cause a complete breakdown in the interpersonal relationship of the interview. At the first evidence of aggression, the operator should endeavor to search back for soft points of insecurity that have not been previously used. These areas of insecurity should then be directed at the subject to sidetrack his aggression. An example of this method is:

I. Are you married?
S. No, I'm divorced.

I. You're divorced?
S. Yes, my husband was no good.

I. Your husband was no good?
S. The dirty rat abused me.

I. He abused you?
S. He beat me up and took off with another woman.

I. He took off with another woman?
S. All men are like that—all they want to do is use a woman (first appearance of aggression).

I. All they want to do is use a woman?
S. That's right. You give them everything and when they have taken your youth and good years, they leave (insecurity exhibited).

I. They take your youth and leave?
S. Yes, and mistreat you in the process.

I. And mistreat you in the process?
S. You bet. All men are liars and rats (more aggression).

I. You must find it difficult to adjust socially, now that you are alone. Do you have any definite plans for the future?
S. I don't know (stricken with insecurity), but . . . etc.

Rogerian technique does not seem to work well in those criminal matters where the offender has been conditioned to a "Yes" or "No" answer pattern by previous interrogations. The method is, however, quite effective at the interview level for ascertaining hidden resentments.

The most important salient feature recognizable about person-ality guilt is that it exists as a part of the human organism. Once this is realized, and the tool of insecurity to increase internal stress is brought into play, its place in the scheme of interviewing can be detected. We recall the story of a subnormal fellow who was banging his head against the side of a building. When asked why, he said, "Because it feels so good when I stop." Relief of guilt or expiation feels good. Understanding and rationalization are the prime tools for producing relief. The subject is waiting for some sense of relief, and when it is forthcoming, he associates it with the rapport he associates with the interviewer. Personal guilt and the anxiety it produces can be restarted and relieved; that is, in effect, a process that closely duplicates Pavlovian conditioning. Continu-ous use of the process causes the subject to become dependent upon the interviewer. This dependence on the interviewer for understanding becomes almost drug-like. Later, through the use of proper questioning technique, virtually all derogatory information can be elicited. Even in the case of the most heinous crimes, if this technique is adequately maintained throughout the course of the interrogation, the subject will have an overwhelming need for relief and expiation which he believes *only the interviewer can furnish.*

10

BREAKTHROUGH

10

BREAKTHROUGH

A. DEFINED

The breakthrough is that point in the interview/interrogation when the first admission (no matter how small) is furnished. During World War II, German General Rommell, prior to the invasion of Europe by the Allies, said: "In order to stop them, we must do it at the beaches." Once the interviewer/interrogator possesses one admission, the "beachhead" is established.

To illustrate, we know a fellow who propositioned a girl, asking: "Will you go to bed with me for two million dollars?" She said: "For two million dollars? Well of course." He then asked: "How about, then, for two dollars?" She indignantly replied: "What do you think I am?" He answered: "We've already established that; actually, we're quibbling over price."

From an investigative standpoint, the subject's one admission, no matter how small, establishes that he was at the scene of the crime, participated in the crime in some way, etc., etc., etc. When talking to a cookie thief, this question becomes more of a statement of fact than a question: "Have you ever stolen a cookie?" It relates to the two million dollars mentioned in the earlier story: "Now, how about a box of cookies? A case of cookies? A carload of cookies?" The point is that it is logical to assume that we have all stolen a cookie, or at least the cookie thief has stolen a cookie. Once this admission is established, *the quantity of cookies is merely a supporting detail.*

B. THE "BUY SIGNS"

Salesmen often talk about the "buy signs," which are those physio/psycho responses that subtly tell them that the prospect is ready to close. During interviews and interrogations, a very similar set of buy signs exists, although the language may be different.

During an interrogation, the most common buy sign encountered is: "I am not saying I did this thing, but if I did, what could happen to me?" The next most common buy sign, and also the most common form of self-betrayal, is when the subject denies an allegation that has never been mentioned.

In the authors' experience, we believe there is some physiological link between the right arm and deception. About every fifth subject interviewed/interrogated by us, who is of the "very emotional" classification, denies by raising his right hand and in an impassioned way says: "My right to God if I have done this!" Usually after such an emotional outburst, the interviewer/interrogator should pay particular attention to the exact verbiage of the next words spoken by the subject, for it is here that this subject will present his first line of defense and most probably present a defense directed to the specific area of stress that disturbs him most. May we note that this is why specific allegations are never discussed with a subject during the beginning of an interview/interrogation.

Beyond the "Yes" attitude or mood, the buy signs are variables. The interviewer/interrogator actually feels them by relating to his subject. The investigator who has no feeling toward his subject will never be able to identify these buy signs, which are different and quite apart from the submissive attitude mentioned in Chapters 6 and 8.

There may be times the buy sign is bypassed. One of these very special (and rare) cases when this occurs is called "ego sealing." It is best exemplified by the interrogation of a hardened Mafia-connected suspect in a highjacking case conducted by one of the authors. This Mafioso had been arrested on numerous occasions and was well conditioned to give only "Yes" or "No" answers. He knew that he only had to wait four to five hours prior to being released. Because of his employment, the suspect had to sit through the interrogation. The interrogator adopted the following strategy:

First, preliminary information was taken from the suspect by a different interviewer. Then, the suspect was brought to the location of phase #2 of the interview, where the interrogator was sitting behind the desk doing imaginary paper work. The subject was then told to sit in a chair well away from the interrogator (on the other side of the room) with the comment: "Sit there quietly. Don't disturb me; I am busy with other work right now." After about twenty minutes, the subject began to fidget and started to protest his innocence. Before the protestation of innocence could be completed, the interrogator cut off the protestation with the comment: "Just sit there and be quiet; I don't believe that you participated in this highjacking anyhow."

Later, at appropriate intervals and every time the subject attempted to speak or assert himself, the interrogator commented: "You could not have done it"—"You are too stupid to have done it"—"This job took a lot of planning, and you are not capable of that type of thinking"—"There had to be a lot of loyalty from the other people involved, and you could not have inspired that"— "You don't have the mental capability to think out something like this"—and on and on until, after about an hour, the suspect came over to the interrogator's desk and began pounding on it with both fists, screaming in complete emotional submission: "I did it. I can prove it, and you—you lousy s.o.b., what right have you to say that I am too stupid to have done it?"

The pressure of completely sealing off the ego was, of course, the cause of this outburst of self-denouncement. Thereafter, the subject had to be given to another interrogator for expansion of details about the admission. The subject later pled guilty to the highjacking charge.

Once the various buy signs appear, how does the investigator capitalize on them? There are two very popular methods: One is by citing all the facts in summary form and diverting the subject's attention from a breakthrough admission by seeking motive. For example: "I know how you did "X," "Y," and "Z"—perhaps it would be in your best interest to tell my why." The other method is to create a verbal vacuum: "I know that you did this, and I will not allow you to put yourself in the awkward position of lying to me"—"If you are not willing to be completely truthful with me, then I advise you to say absolutely nothing." This will be followed by what may seem to be an eternity of silence. The rule here is that after a verbal vacuum has been created, usually *he who speaks first is the loser.* Wait your subject out, and he will probably say: "Okay, what do you want to know?"

C. THE BLUFF

Throughout this book, we have scrupulously avoided such words as "trickery" and "bluffing," mainly because of the old mystery story concept of the detective creating a false situation which would entrap the suspect into a dramatic admission of guilt. Such a conception could cause a false impression of this practice as a mainstay of the interrogative art.

Bluffs or staged situations are sometimes used, but dependence on them should be avoided. We find that an investigator who has not properly prepared for the interview/interrogation more often has to resort to the bluff or make use of staged situations.

Bluffing is essentially an expansion technique where a high percentage of known facts are available to the interrogator, which will decrease any chance that the subject will know that a bluff is being used. As a general rule, bluffing or staged situations should never be used to obtain the initial breakthrough admission. Once the subject detects the bluff as guess work, all control and rapport will break down. How do you feel when you know that you have been used?

When the investigation is shoddy or inferences are regarded as facts, subsequent interrogation that has no firm foundation will be regarded by subjects as just more bluffing.

D. FURNISHING RELIEF

There are only two physiological systems basically: those that deal with pain, and those that deal with pleasure. *There is nothing pleasurable about being interrogated.* Because of this premise, all interrogation and some interviewing must be considered as a threat to the wellbeing of the human organism. Merely asking a question produces a threat to the wellbeing—or stress, as we have pointed out in the preceding chapter.

Furnishing expiation or atonement is not the same as providing relief from immediate stress. Let us go back to our earlier example of "breakthrough: "Have you ever stolen a cookie?" The subject answers "Yes," thinking that he would be silly not to reveal this very human act. Let's analyze the emotions involved in "Yes, I have stolen a cookie. First the subject feels that if he does not admit this, they will believe him to be completely uncooperative. Second, the theft of a cookie is of no consequence, so it won't make any difference. Third, he thinks: "Now that I have admitted it (theft of a cookie), why do I feel guilty?"

The above analysis follows closely the formation of normal personality insecurity and its translation by the infant into guilt feelings. The questioning, "What have I done?" becomes the guilty, "I have done." This guilt, immediately brought on by the admission of the theft of a cookie, produces stress (however small the quantity of goods). Relief of this stress is what we are seeking.

A simple "So what!" is the most powerful relief-furnishing tool known to the interviewer/interrogator. "You lied about your income tax—so what! doesn't everybody?" "You smuggled a bottle of liquor in—so what! doesn't everybody?" "You took home some office supplies—so what! doesn't everybody?" "You cheated on the test—so what! hasn't everybody at some time?" "You hit him in the mouth—so what! didn't he have it coming?" "You smoked some grass—so what, doesn't everybody?" And on, and on, and on with the rationale, "So what!"

We hope, then, somewhere within the "So what!" examples that we have been able to furnish the reader with a quantity of relief, and if you felt it, possibly you can visualize a subject under parallel conditions also obtaining relief. If the relief is furnished to the stress caused by the initial breakthrough admission, then we have fullfilled the early requirements in part of the "conditioned reflex."

Sometimes, prior to the relief of stress, one can induce stress. For example; "I don't want you to be nervous about what I am going to say." That, in effect, produces the very nervousness that the interviewer/interrogator has denied wanting to produce.

Another very common method of furnishing relief to stress occurs just prior to breakthrough. It is a method known in sales techniques as "Taking the wind out of their sails" and involves stating every defense to the breakthrough admission prior to the subject's being allowed such a defense. Most humans have an innate sense of fairness which derives from the sense of order found in other mammals. There is a definite eating order among animals, from felines through primates. All primates seem to show some concept of fairness. For the purposes of interviewing and interrogation, this sense of fairness in the human, (in addition to the human's natural laziness which may appear as the copying of another's thoughts), can be capitalized on by stating first the premise, then the defense, and then the reasons that the defenses will fail. The salesman, in using the "Taking the wind out of their sails" technique, overcomes sales resistance by verbalizing the defenses before the prospect does. For example: "I know that you are thinking that you can't afford this, but our monthly payment system is so small that you need not think of the total amount."

Examples of this technique applied to interviewing/interrogation are: "I sense that you are thinking that you really don't want to get involved by furnishing a description of the event we are discussing, but your mere presence on the scene has already involved you"—or, "You are probably thinking that by freely discussing this matter, you will put yourself into a jail, but your involvement was so slight that common sense should tell you, you will probably only get a reprimand"—or, "So you stole a cookie and it worries you—so what! doesn't everybody steal cookies?"

The very fact that you stated the stressful issue, the subject's defense which would produce more stress, and the ineffectiveness of the defense, prior to the subject's use of these verbalizations, places him in the position of having to undergo all the emotions associated with stress and stress relief without necessarily saying anything. You, in effect, are in complete control of the subject's emotions, and so long as you are aware of this, you will maintain that control. Lose sight of this or be unaware of it, however, and control will be lost not only of the subject's emotions, but the entire course of the interview/interrogation.

E. RE-ESTABLISHING STRESS

After a breakthrough and the furnishing of relief, it is necessary to reestablish stress and re-relieve it a number of times so as to establish a pattern of psychological dependence and to fulfill the requirements of the "conditioned reflex." The "conditioned reflex" that we wish to utilize in interviewing and interrogating is:

Stimulas	Interviewer/interrogator empathy, subject's stress, subject's guilt feelings.
Response	Relief of subject's stress, feeling of well-being (expiation or atonement).
Associated Stimulas	Feedback of stress points and stress release.
Associated Response	Dependence upon interviewer/interrogator for stress relief.
Byproduct	Information.

You can see by the above behavior picture that reestablishment of stress and the process of stress relief are merely repetition of the original stimulus response, but the magnitude is gradually increased. For example: "Did you ever steal a cookie? a box of cookies? a case of cookies? a truckload of cookies?"

We should also like to note that from the psychological point of view, information derived during an interrogation is only a byproduct of the established "conditioned reflex." Even though the discovery of new stress points may be synonymous with information gathering, the real end objective is forming the "conditioned reflex." If the re-establishment of stress involves an increasing spiral of stress points, then it would follow that relief to each stress point must be equally ascending.

May we also note that in our combined interrogation experience we have never gotten the complete story of anything at an initial breakthrough. In fact, during World War II, the training of spies on both sides included the polishing of the normal defense of a story within a story. The spy was taught to admit on being captured not that he was a spy, but rather that he was a philandering husband escaping the wrath of his wife. Later, he admitted to being a petty thief; still later, a burglar running from the police; and, following that, a murderer. All these cover stories were designed to avoid the real issue of the subject's involvement in espionage.

At an unconscious level, we all tend to form lines or levels of defense, and these levels seem to correspond with the value structure of the individual. As the spy had a totally false series of cover stories, so does the average person form perimeters of defense and stress. "Do you have any feelings about stealing a cookie? How about a box? a case? a truckload?" If we were investigating the highjacking of a truckload of cookies, then the ascending levels of stress can easily be visualized.

F. DANGERS OF OVERCONDITIONING

The cases of persons giving false confessions to please the interrogator are so numerous that examples are unnecessary. The human mechanism is fragile; and, as we have seen from the forming of a conditioned reflex, it is possible to go too far, creating a byproduct of false information or a false confession.

There also comes a point in any interview/interrogation at which further questioning will result in diminished returns. To avoid overconditioning, the investigator must be completely aware that he does have a vested interest in gaining a confession, either as a part of his record of arrests or commerically because he can command more status or future remuneration. *Once aware is twice warned.*

The easiest method of preventing overconditioning has been described in Chapter 7, when we advised, "Test all assertions." As a general rule, any testimony that is uncorroborated is suspect. That is why even confessions, when uncorroborated, are not usually admissible as evidence.

During a commercial interrogation, there is no practical purpose for a $25 to $100 an hour interrogator to continue an interrogation for an additional time period after he has established the necessary intelligence. This is one point of diminishing returns.

The conditioned reflex, especially as formed during an interrogation, distorts the original concepts of reality. It would be most inhuman to get a person, via the conditioned reflex, to furnish information that would limit his employment, freedom, or even life without at least readjusting that person's concepts to the new reality that exists after the information has been furnished.

We know of interrogators who have had subjects who committed suicide after furnishing confessions. This is, of course, the extreme; but you have changed reality and the future course of events by persuading your subject to furnish self-incriminating testimony. It then becomes your moral obligation, as a fellow human being, to try to aid this subject's psychological re-adjustment to the changed reality. You have no responsibility for the crime he committed, but surely you are responsible for helping him to face and accept any consequences that may arise as a result of the testimony he furnished you!

11

EVIDENCE

11

EVIDENCE

A. CLASSIFICATIONS

All squares are rectangles, but not all rectangles are squares. All interviewing and interrogation results in testimony's being given, but not all the testimony given is necessarily furnished to a court. Most testimony taken in investigation will never come into play in courtroom procedure; however, for the sake of this book, it is best to remember that all interviews, interrogation, and/or other investigative work—whether it be criminal surveillance or even for personnel procedures—may at some future time come under the scrutiny of some official body. It is obvious that criminal and civil litigation may call forth scrutiny by appellate courts, but certainly the personnel interviewer should be aware that his work may be thoroughly examined by the NLRB, a state unemployment board, a state safety board, or some other regulatory agency. Therefore, the objective of any investigation—i.e., interview/interrogation—is the development of evidence via the route of testimony.

In ancient times, there were neither trial nor courtroom procedures as they exist today. Commission of a crime was determined primarily by oath and torture. The oath descends from ordeal; in fact, even today among uncivilized tribes throughout the world, one who swears by oath in many cases will actually call down a curse upon himself should he not relate the facts as they were. Gradually, our civilization discarded the crude and inhuman methods of determining commission of an act, such as trial by ordeal, and adopted judges. Later, civilization added tribunals; and, still later, juries under the guidance of judges were the determiners of fact. Early jurists discovered that they had to have some form of order to enable them to dispose of evidence which was untrustworthy or inaccessible so that the jury would hear "only truth."

There are no universal rules of evidence. Ruling of what constitutes evidence may pretty generally be considered the same, but how evidence is handled may vary from jurisdiction to jurisdiction or regulatory body to regulatory body. A clear-cut example of this is the testimony that may be inadmissible in a criminal trial may be admissible in an arbitration of one sort or another or in civil litigation. Every interviewer/interrogator should become intimately familiar with rules of evidence of whatever regulatory body may eventually scrutinize the end results of his work.

The legal definition of evidence[1] is: Any means by which any alleged matter of fact, the truth of which is submitted to investigation, is established or disproved. This definition is quite broad, and it leads us to three major classifications of evidence, which are: (1) Direct Evidence, (2) Circumstantial Evidence, and (3) Physical Evidence.

1. A witness testifying "I saw such and such occur" is providing *direct evidence.* An example would be:

> A man on the witness stand says that at approximately 2:00 p.m. on the afternoon of a specified day, while walking in a given direction down a specified street, he saw a man identified as John Smith, driving a red automobile with an identified license number, run over the curb and drive right through a plate-glass window, perhaps thirty feet from him.

2. *Circumstantial Evidence.* Let us suppose our witness testified that he was standing on the street at 2:00 p.m. on a given day, facing northward, when he heard a tremendous crash, where-

---

[1]No. 1, *Greenleaf on Evidence,* Chapter 1, Section 1: "Evidence" probably stems from the word "evidencia," "clear, clearness." Hence the idea of evidence as "a means of proof, to make evident, to bring light."

upon he immediately turned around and saw the front end of the red automobile, with the identified license number, pushed through the plate-glass window, with John Smith still at the wheel, and it was established in prior testimony that the witness had just passed the plate-glass window and not noticed an automobile sticking through it. That would be circumstantial evidence, sometimes called indirect evidence. The fact that the witness did not see the act but that the circumstances were such that he saw virtually all the contributory factors and/or the resultant factors, is circumstantial evidence. Direct evidence, as we have shown, is testimony encompassing the immediate experience of the witness; circumstantial evidence is testimony which, because of circumstance, involves logical inference.

Circumstantial evidence is generally admissible because[2]:

> Crimes are secret. Most men, conscious of criminal purpose and about the execution of criminal acts, seek the security of secrecy or darkness. It is therefore necessary to use all other modes of evidence besides that of direct testimony, provided such proofs may be relied on as leading to safe and satisfactory conclusions; and thanks to a beneficent providence, the laws of nature and relations of things to each other are so linked and combined together, that a medium of proof is often thereby furnished, leading to inferences and conclusions as strong as those arising from direct testimony.

There is always some area of doubt brought about by circumstantial evidence; and although the circumstantial evidence may have a very high level of definition regarding the act in question, it never quite seems to reach the credibility level of direct evidence. Our constant reminder to test all assertions is based on this specific, fundamental difference between the direct and the circumstantial, and any interviewer/interrogator must approach all circumstantial evidence with extreme caution, for here human phantasy can play many tricks.

3. *Physical evidence* is evidence which speaks for itself and requires no explanation whatsoever, merely identification. Such evidence has extremely broad range of coverage and, although

[2]*Commonwealth vs. Webster*, 59 Massachusetts, 295, 311 (1850).

subordinate to direct evidence in its level of credibility, may sometimes have greater weight in the minds of an examining body—for example, fingerprints upon a murder weapon; video tapes or other photographic evidence of a bank holdup; possession of loot derived from a burglary. There are cases on record where the aroma of whiskey and the sound of music were admitted as physical evidence. Photographs, moving pictures, video and audio tape-recordings, X-rays, maps, diagrams, handwriting, typewriting, tool marks, tire marks, experiments and tests conducted in court, personal notes, and bruises and contusions are examples of physical evidence.

B. ADMISSIBILITY AND WEIGHT

The rules of evidence apparently seek to protect the jury from improper evidence without necessarily insuring any given result. These rules of evidence are, therefore, concerned with the admissibility of facts and pertinency of materials—not with their weight. Weight of evidence is a question to be determined only by the fact-finders.

An example of weight would be that a crime is committed and the suspect brings forth an alibi wherein his mother testifies that he was at home and in bed at the the time the act occurred; and a second alibi witness is a physician who was attending the suspect in his home. Certainly, both witnesses, the mother and the physician, would be giving admissible testimony; however, it is probable that a jury or fact-finding body would attach more weight to the testimony of the disinterested physician than to the testimony of the mother.

Interviewers/interrogators and others concerned with investigations should generally seek evidence with the greatest weight; and in fact, relating back to our discussion of undermining confidence in Chapter 8, it should be noted that one cannot use lightly-weighted evidence to overcome a high degree of confidence in a witness. As a general rule, the investigator should always seek evidence of the greatest possible weight.

C. RELEVANCY AND IRRELEVANCY

The relation to the matter at hand of the evidence, or the bearing that a fact has upon an issue as to proving its truth or untruth, is the relevancy of the evidence. If evidence does not show truth or untruth, probability or improbability, then it is irrelevant. Any fact which logically aids in determining the truth, unless specifically excluded by some rule or principle of law, would be considered relevant. Some of the matters that are usually considered relevant are:

1. Motive.

2. Capability.

3. Opportunity.

4. Expressions or utterances before the fact.

5. The means of commission.

6. Circumstances and conditions attendant.

7. Demeanor and behavior after the fact.

8. Resisting or avoiding interview/interrogation/arrest.

9. Concealment of identity, capability, or other pertinent evidence.

10. Manufactured or false evidence.

11. Attempted suicide.

12. Escape or attempted escape.

13. Confessions.

14. Confessions and contributory circumstances.

15. Other contributory circumstances.

Everything that we have referred to above can be found if every one of the "Seven W's" (as discussed in Chapter 2) can be answered and weighty evidence attached.

D. MATERIALITY AND IMMATERIALITY

This is an abstract area of law in so far as not all relevant evidence is necessarily material. If a body of fact-finders allowed all relevant evidence however slight and inconsequential, then the trial of facts before that body might be unending. "The essence of remoteness is such: A want of open and visible connection between the evidenciary and principal facts, that all things considered the former are not worthy or safe to be admitted in the proof of the latter."[3]

Although a fact may have a direct bearing on a case, if it has such little value as to be worthless of proof, it is immaterial. In our earlier referred-to automobile accident, the color of the steering wheel in the already identified car would thus be immaterial. Materiality of evidence is for the court or factfinding body to decide. Therefore, interviewers/interrogators should never attempt "to play lawyer" by omitting a fact because they believe it to be immaterial. The posture of the interviewer/interrogator and all other investigators is to develop the facts, to report on them, and to present them to the interested parties.

E. COMPETENCY AND INCOMPETENCY

1. *Of Evidence.* For evidence to be admissible, it must not only be relevant and material to the issues, but it must also be competent. Competent evidence must be legally adquate and sufficient. Legal adequacy and sufficiency are different from pertinency or importance. Examples of competency are:

   a. That a photograph is only competent if it is first shown that the photograph truly and accurately portrays the subject matter reproduced in the photograph.

   b. Another example of competency or incompetency would be an attempt to elicit the cause of death from a layman. It is obvious that only a person trained in medicine and pathology could present an opinion as to the cause of death. No matter how experienced the average layman is, it would be difficult to overcome a lack of background or training to show he had competency in deriving an opinion.

2. *Of witnesses.* The competency of evidence is very closely associated with the competency of witnesses. For example, witnesses may be declared incompetent because of emotional connections, material relationships, personal motivations and bias, or because they are too young or legally insane.

---

[3]*State vs. Kelly,* 77 Connecticut, 266, 58A705 (1904).

At common law, insane persons were ipso facto disqualified. That is no longer the case. The general rule is that a person affected with insanity is competent as a witness if he has sufficient understanding to comprehend the obligation of an oath and is capable of giving a correct account of the matters seen or heard in reference to the facts in issue.[4]

A child may prove to be an all-important witness. The alert mind of a child may envision a situation an adult may have overlooked completely. Moreover, the influence that a child's testimony may have on a jury is well known.[5]

Testimony of husband and wife, either for or against in a criminal case, was not permitted under the common law; however, modern legislation has modified this rule so that one spouse is usually considered competent to testify for the other in most all jurisdictions. The testimony against the other spouse is a totally different situation, and that varies from state to state. In some states, the spouse may testify but is not compellable.

The interviewer/interrogator should always know the test of competency for whatever state or jurisdiction his work may eventually come to rest in.

F. OTHER TESTS OF ADMISSIBILITY

Although there are numerous other tests of admissibility, these have no real bearing on interviewing and interrogation, so we only include a few of them here for their academic interest.

Courts will usually reject evidence which tends to raise new issues not connected. Sometimes evidence will be disqualified because it is unduly prejudicial. Evidence that a defendant has been convicted of other crimes is usually rejected, except under very special circumstances.

Issues involving peculiarities of a litigant's family, religious, or racial inclinations, are usually omitted on the same grounds. Privileged communication is normally rejected in most jurisdictions (privileged communications are those between lawyer and

---

[4]*Commonwealth vs. Koch*, 305 Pennsylvania, 146, 157A479 (1931).

[5]*State vs. Seberger*, 131 Connecticut, 546, 41A2d, 101, 157ALR1355 (1945).

client, medical doctor and patient, priest and confessor, and, in some jurisdictions, private investigator and client).

There are other tests of admissibility, but the primary and fundamental rule is that evidence must be relevant, material, and competent.

G. JUDICIAL NOTICE

There are certain facts which are accepted as true without necessity of proof. Usually in those instances, fact-finding bodies, such as courts, will take judicial notice of them. It is certainly well known that state courts will take notice of their own laws and those of the federal government, and that the federal courts will notice the statutes of many of the states if attention is called to them.

As a general rule, the statutes of one state will not be judicially noticed by courts of another state. Presently, a number of states within their statutes provide that they shall be noticed by other courts as well.

Matters of fact that are judicially noticed cover a huge range of subject matter, such as:

1. Matters of general knowledge—that certain diseases are contagious, and that tires when skidding usually leave skid marks.

2. The qualities of matter—the explosive or flammable nature of gasoline.

3. Laws of nature—such as the time of rising and setting of the sun in particular areas.

4. Scientific facts and principles—the speed of light or of sound, or mathematical formula for determining speed from skid marks.

5. Geographic facts—the location of cities, towns, or various boundaries.

6. Historical facts—in the United States, presidential elections are during leap years.

7. Abbreviations for words or phrases—"D.V.M." is generally accepted as a "Doctor of Veterinary Medicine" and "M.D." as a Doctor of Medicine."

8. Weights and measures—there are sixteen ounces to an avoirdupois pound and three feet to a yard.

9. The political organization of federal, state, and local governments—census reports and similar facts.

The importance of judicial notice is not fully appreciated, but decisions are frequently sustained or reversed because judicial notice of certain facts was not taken. For example, there have been a number of times that burglary convictions were overturned because the statute and indictment read "Burglary in the Night" and the complaining witness did not discover the matter until well after daybreak.

H. THE BURDEN OF PROOF

In the United States, no person may be convicted of a criminal act unless the prosecution presents evidence necessary for that conviction or the defendant pleads guilty. The burden of proof in the trial, and hence in the investigation, always rests on the prosecution. That burden never varies.

In civil litigation, the plaintiff only has to establish his case by a preponderance of the evidence; which means that the plaintiff's evidence merely has to outweigh the defendant's evidence, whereas in criminal cases the prosecution has the burden of proving the defendant guilty beyond a reasonable doubt.

All of this does not mean that the defendant never has to prove his own allegations. There are defenses—such as insanity, alibi, and self-defense—where the defendant must affirm and present collateral evidence to support his defense. There is almost no accord between courts as to the amount of proof required in such cases. One thing is certain: The jury and/or the judge must believe the posture of the defendant; therefore, it is necessary to present an adequate defense if the jury and/or the judge is to be persuaded that the posture of the defendant is correct.

I. THE "HEARSAY RULE" AND ITS EXCEPTIONS

It would be ideal if a criminal act under trial by a fact-finding body were witnessed by the judge and jury, but of course this is impossible, so evidence is brought forth to attempt to show the guilt of the individual accused of committing the act. As a protection against false testimony, various rules regarding hearsay and their exceptions developed.

"Hearsay" signifies all evidence which is not founded upon the personal knowledge of the witness from whom it is elicited and which consequently does not depend wholly for its credibility and weight on the confidence which the court or jury may have in him. Hearsay evidence is information that is relayed from another person to the witness before it reaches the ears of the court or jury. The basic reason that hearsay evidence is inadmissible is that the original witness may not be available for cross-examination.

There are very sound reasons as to why courts will not permit hearsay testimony. One is, of course, the high degree of error in the transmission of information. Another reason is the common-law idea that the defendant has a right to be confronted by his accuser; and, of course, a third reason is that a judge or jury, in evaluating the testimony of any witness, should be able to judge critically his demeanor and attitudes while presenting testimony.

The hearsay rule applies not only to oral statements, but to written statements as well. The fact that some statements and all affidavits are made under oath does not affect application of the hearsay rule; they are still hearsay and will not be admitted. There are, however, reasons why statements and affidavits should be taken.

Once having given a statement, the witness realizes it would be imprudent to make contradictory statements later. Although the statement cannot be used directly, it may be used as a basis for impeachment or possible prosecution for perjury. A statement or affidavit can always be used to refresh the memory of a witness who says he does not remember.

There are exceptions to the hearsay rule which exist because of certain protective circumstances surrounding them, and they are:

1. Confessions and Admissions

All confessions and admissions are hearsay. The two basic reasons that confessions and admissions are admitted into evidence as exceptions to the hearsay rule are:

a. The judicial reasoning that an accused person *volunteering* information *against* his or her self-interest is probably telling the truth.

b. The weight and importance that a confession or admission has in the process of accomplishing justice.

There is a legal definition of confession, which is that: "An accused person knowingly makes an acknowledgement that he or she committed or participated in commission of the criminal act. This acknowledgement must be broad enough to comprehend every essential element necessary to make out a case against the defendant."[6]

There is also a substantial difference between a confession and an admission against interest or an "incriminating statement" as defined by Wharton.[7] By this definition, an admission contains one or more facts constituting the criminal act, from which guilt or participation can be inferred but does not necessarily follow. For example, a confession would be, "I shot John!" An admission against interest would be: "I was alone in the room with John at the time he was shot."

Every jurisdiction must have voluntariness as a prerequisite to admissibility of a confession. Not all jurisdictions require showing the voluntary nature of admissions against interest.

There are two forms of confessions:

a. The judicial confession, which comprises guilty pleas before judicial bodies and a number of other circumstances, such as, confession before grand jury, coroner's jury, military court of inquiry. We mention this form of confession because the circumstances surrounding the judicial confession are special and might, in an ordinary interrogation, come up, thus changing the later admissibility of any confession obtained.

Requirements of the judicial confession are that the defendant before having made the statement or plea constituting the confession shall have been cautioned that he had a right to remain silent; that he was under no legal obligation to speak or in any way to offer self-incrimination; that if he or

---

[6]James vs. State, 86 Georgia, App. 282, 71, S.E. 2d 568 (1952).

[7]*Criminal Evidence*, p. 954, 11th edition: "A confession is an acknowledgement in express terms by a party in a criminal case, of his guilt of the crime charged, while an admission is a statement by the accused direct or implied of facts pertinent to the issue and tending in connection with other facts tending to prove his or her guilt."

she did testify or make any self-incriminating statement, it must be entirely and totally voluntary; and that anything he or she said during the self-incriminating statement or testimony would be used against the defendant in future judicial process. Also, the defendant must not have been under judicial compulsion because of the awe-inspiring surroundings or solemnity of the occasion. It must be clear, in the defendant's mind, that a legal proceeding is not an inquisition.

b. All other confessions are extra-judicial. Confessions made before apprehension and in arrest or after are extra-judicial. These are the type that the interviewer/interrogator deals with most frequently.

The validity of an extra-judicial confession may be tested by determining the voluntariness, the presence of inducement, pressure of indigence, and pressure of authority. Extra-judicial confessions are generally admissible, even though they are:

a. Gained through trickery or deceit.

b. Unwritten.

c. Unsigned.

d. Not made under oath.

e. Not signed or attested to by witnesses.

f. Made without benefit of advice of legal counsel; however, the offer of counsel in some circumstances must have been made. The present law as defined by the Supreme Court of the United States implies that custody begins at that point where the accused is asked to accompany an officer of the court to a place of authority. We note that this attitude in no way and in no jurisdiction affects the private agent or citizen. Thereafter, the Supreme Court has held that extra-judicial confessions made to officers of the court, including all law-enforcement officers, shall be subject to the rules of judicial confession.[8] Therefore, an extra-judicial confession, whether

---

[8]*Escabedo vs. Illinois,* 378 US 478. *Miranda vs. Arizona,* 384 US 436. Johnson vs. New Jersey, 384 US 719.

given to an enforcement officer or private citizen, and in order to be admissible, must show voluntariness; must show that it was not induced by threats of harmful consequences; must show that there was no undue psychological pressure (an example would be persistent questioning by relays of interrogators); must show that there was no promise of reward, either present or future, and even the intimation of promise or inducement would invalidate a confession.

Your authors believe that the private citizen, in receiving an extra-judicial confession, should adhere to the judicial confession rules as a guide, mainly in the interest of humane treatment, fair play, and justice.

Where, in an interview/interrogation of a detected and apprehended shoplifter through a private citizen (store employee), the confession and written statement obtained by reason of inducement—such as, "Sign this statement and I won't prosecute"—the inducement to confess would be clearcut. What may not be so clearcut is the fact that the alleged shoplifter may be innocent and a false confession may have been elicited.

To summarize, judicial confession rules require, in addition to voluntariness, lack of threats or promises, no undue psychological pressures, and the advising of the constitutional rights and guarantees. Those constitutional rights are:

a. Right to remain silent.

b. Right to have an attorney present and to speak to an attorney prior to any questioning of a custodial nature.

c. Knowledge that if the suspect cannot afford to hire a lawyer, one will be appointed to represent him before any questioning, if he so wishes.

d. Anything that the suspect says of a self-incriminatory nature can and will be used against him in a court of law.

Confessions gained through deception or from intoxicated persons are not usually inadmissible, provided the elements of voluntariness are still present. Although the confession of an intoxicated person may be admissible if the voluntariness is evident, the real deciding factor of admissibility is the competence of the person making the confession at the time the confession is offered.

2. Tacit Admissions

The rules of evidence recognize admissions against interest that are said and *unsaid.* This means that a suspect may incriminate himself not only by direct statements, but also by declarations or behavior by which he or she implicitly admits the truth of any charges against him or her. Thus, silence in the face of an accusation of a crime may constitute conduct or circumstances from which an admission of guilt may be inferred.

Therefore, as a general rule:

> When a statement tending to involve one in the commission of a crime which is made in his presence and hearing and such statement is not denied, contradicted, or objected to by him, both the statement and the fact of his failure to deny it are admissible against him as evidence of his acquiescence in its truth.[9]

> The basis of such rule is that the natural reaction of one accused of the commission of a crime or of implication therein is to deny the accusation if it is unjust or unfounded. The hearsay character of the incriminating statement made to the accused would render it inadmissible except for the fact that the statement is not offered in evidence as proof of a fact asserted but as a predicate to the showing of the reaction of the accused thereto.[10]

The recognized tests of admissibility of tacit admissions are:

    a. The accusation must be made in the presence of the defendant.

    b. He must have understood that he was being accused of complicity in a crime.

    c. The statement must be such as would naturally provoke a denial from one similarly situated.

    d. The circumstances must have been such as to afford the accused the opportunity to act and speak freely.

---

[9] *Am. Jur., Evidence,* Sec. 570.

e. The person accused must have remained silent or made an evasive or equivocal reply short of a total denial.

f. The language of the accusation must be shown in its entirety and in the words used by the accuser.

g. If the accused does make a denial to the accusation, neither his denial nor the accusation is admissible.

3. Conversations in the Presence of the Defendant

Where a statement adversely affecting the party or his rights is made in his presence and hearing, so that he understands it and the statement is such as would naturally call for a denial if it were not true, the statement and his failure to deny are admissible as tending to show his concession of its truth, provided such evidence is relevant and material to an issue in the case.[10] However, incriminatory remarks overheard by a person during conversation between others in his presence are not admissible when he denies them because, as in the case of tacit admissions, there can be no implied admission of the truth of a statement which an accused unequivocally denies or clearly shows by his conduct that he does not acquiesce in it.[11]

4. Dying Declarations

In the criminal law, the term "dying declaration" is a statement made:

a. By the victim of a homicide.

b. While about to die.

c. In expectation of death and without any hope of recovery.

d. Concerning the facts and circumstances under which the fatal injury was inflicted.

A dying declaration is admissible only in a trial for homicide of the person charged with having caused the death of the declarant.[12] As the New York Court of Appeals said:

---

[10] *20 Am. Jur., Evidence*, Sec. 575,; 31 *C.J.S. Evidence*, Sec. 294, pp. 1057-1060.

[11] *State vs. Bryant*, 235 N.C. 420, 70 S.E. 2d 186 (1952).

[12] *People vs. Buettner*, 233 Ill. 272, 84 N.E. 218, 13 Am. Cas. 235 (1908).

The belief that "a dying man is ever presumed to speak the truth" is ancient. (See 5 Wigmore on Evidence, sec. 1430, p. 219, et. seq. (3rd Ed.). As Wigmore says (sec. 1438, p. 230): "All courts have agreed, with more of less difference of language, that the approach of death produces a state of mind in which the utterances of the dying person are to be taken as free from all ordinary motives to misstate." The great dramatist Shakespeare expressed the common feeling long before it was sanctioned by judicial opinion (King John, Act V, sc. 4). A classical statement of the principle is found in Woodcock's Case (Leach Cr. Law, p. 500 (4th Ed.) (1789): "The general principle on which this species of evidence (dying declarations) is admitted is that they are declarations made in extremity, when the party is silenced, and the mind is influenced by the most powerful considerations to speak the truth. A situation so solemn and so awful is considered by the law as creating an obligation equal to that which is created by a positive oath administered in a court of justice.[13]

5. Res Gestae Declarations

Res Gestae means "things done." Res Gestae declaration is sometimes called a spontaneous exclamation and covers a situation which presents:

    a. A statling or unusual occurrence.

    b. Sufficient to produce a spontaneous and instinctive reaction.

    c. Under the shock of which certain words are uttered, and

    d. Without the intervention of conscious forethought, reflection, or deliberate design.

Utterances conforming to these requirements, in some way serving to explain, illustrate, or characterize the event, are admissible.[14]

6. Public Records.

7. Regular Entries in the Course of Business.

---

[13]*People vs. Gezzo,* 307 N.Y. 385, 121 N.E. 2d380 (1954).

[14]*20 Am. Jur., Evidence,* secs. 662 et seq.

8. Matters of Pedigree.

9. Former Testimony.

J. Summary

Underlying the admission of all direct, circumstantial, and physical evidence is a fundamental doctrine in the United States known as "the privilege against self-incrimination." The Fifth Amendment, Article Five of the Constitution of the United States, says:

> No person shall be held to answer for a capital, or otherwise infamous crime, unless on a presentation, or indictment of a grand jury, except in cases arising in the land or naval forces or in the militia, when, in actual service in time of war or public danger. Nor shall any person be subject for the same offense to be twice put in jeopardy of life or limb, nor shall be compelled, in any criminal case to be a witness against himself, nor to be deprived of life, liberty or property without due process of law; nor shall private property be taken for public use, without just compensation.

For self-incriminating testimony to be admissible, it must be weighty, relevant, material, competent, given totally voluntarily with no promises or inducements, given in the total absence of the pressures of indigence and judicial authority, given without undue psychological pressure, and given with the subject's awareness that such testimony could and would be used against him in a court of law or other legal proceedings, and given with the awareness of the subject prior to giving testimony that he had the right to talk to a lawyer and have same present with him while giving original testimony.

12

BASIC STATEMENTS

12

BASIC STATEMENTS

A. INTRODUCTION

As we stated at the very outset of the book, the main objective of an interview is for two or more people to get together and discuss something special, and that of an interrogation is the resolution of issues.

Normally, a record of the interview or interrogation is preserved so as to show that the interview actually happened or that the interrogation occurred. These records are usually preserved exactly as given, so that a newspaper reporter, for example, could have the results of his interview published with a minimum of distortions.

It is obvious that any interview or interrogation which might later come under the scrutiny of judicial inquiry should be preserved in some form. Otherwise, the interviewer might die, the subject might die, the interrogator might not be available, the subject might recant, or the subject might change his original testimony. It is, therefore, evident that some organized system should be used in recording the results of an interview or interrogation, and we normally refer to this end product as a statement.

We wish to note that a statement is not necessarily a confession, but rather a basic statement of facts as offered during the interview/interrogation by the interviewee. Many times a statement will be in the form of a confession; however, there are many interview situations where guilt does not even play a part in the end product. Is not an employment application a simple statement of fact about the applicant's background? Does not the applicant, in furnishing a resume which highlights his background, present himself as he wishes the employment interviewer to view him? Naturally, we all know, through vast personal experience, that in writing a resume we are highlighting the best inclusions and deleting all unfavorable information.

Basically, other than the personnel interviewing procedures, all forms of interviewing and interrogation pertain to the development of witnesses, suspects, and subjects where the subsequent testimony may come under judicial scrutiny. In a commercial interview, any fact derived as testimony may play a great part in later settlement of a case. This applies not only to tort actions, but to areas of commercial investigation such as patent investigations.

For example, a witness states he has used a specific product starting at a certain date. This simple fact may prove "prior art" before a patent examiner or a patent court, and large quantities of money may well be at stake on just such testimony. An insurance claim may be adjusted or denied on testimony that might not even be admissible in judicial proceeding.

B. TYPES OF STATEMENTS

As previously noted, a statement is a basic rendering of facts that occurred during an interview/interrogation. In Chapter 11, we learned that admissions were judicially acceptable if they were oral, unsigned, or unsworn as well as other forms of statements. We shall attempt to cover the various forms of statements, briefly:

1. Oral Statements

"Boss, you're full of crap and I quit!" That is a statement! It is oral, clearcut, to the point, and should be preserved exactly as given, because later, in the unemployment compensation hearing, those words may acquire considerable importance in the giving of testimony.

Oral statements are usually taken in personnel interviewing, from various types of witnesses, from suspects, and from subjects.

The most important fact that the interviewer should remember about the oral statement is that, as soon as possible after the oral statement is given, the interviewer should translate it into written form as accurately as he can recall. Naturally, it would be preferable, when taking any oral statement, that there should be another witness in the form of a person or an electronic recording device. In most states, it is legally admissible to record electronically an oral statement without the knowledge or consent of the person making the statement; however, it is admissible in all of the United States where both parties consent to the electronic recording of an oral statement. It should be noted that we are discussing a face-to-face interview only.

The next point, after reducing the recollected oral statement to writing, is corroboration. How shall I corroborate that this oral statement was made to me?

The primary method is another witness: "Boss, you're full of crap and I quit!" At this point, if you are the boss referred to, it would be advisable to get some form of corroboration to this statement; such as, a secretary or a supervisory employee, even if the corroborating witness is brought in after the original oral statement and a second oral statement is made in the form of a tacit admission. For example: "This is your immediate supervisor, and Joe has just told me that I am full of crap and he is going to quit his job. Do you still feel that way?" Joe: "Yes, I do." That is an example of corroboration.

It would be appropiate to have an electronic recording of all conversations with witnesses; however, the philosophic ramifications of this "big brother" atmosphere are such that we do not walk around recording each other's conversations, nor do we recommend routine recording of conversations. However, in preplanning any interview, if a witness is not immediately available, then the second method of corroboration such as an electronic recording, should be made available prior to the interview.

The third method of corroborating an oral statment is an interview log and notes. Notes made during an interview should contain the date of the interview, the name of the person interviewed, and other identifying information. Very important to any judicial scrutiny, within these notes there should be a time log, which may be as simple as the time the interview started to the time concluded, or it may be as complex as noting the times that pertinent remarks and/or admissions are made. A time log is exactly what it says: a log of *usual* occurrences by time. For example, in the notes at a specific time, "Miss Doe, secretary to _____, entered"; or at a specific time, "subject went to the washroom unescorted (or escorted if a custodial situation is involved)." The times of all outgoing phone calls by the subject should be noted, and the time of any incoming phone calls received by the subject during the interview should also be noted. Everything that you consider part of normal living, should be included in the interview log. Log all occurences, unusual as well as usual. To repeat, an interview log is a timed recording in the notes of of all *usual* occurrences plus admissions or pertinent remarks.

From a reporting standpoint, the information developed from an oral statement should be formalized in either a memorandum to the file or in report form, or in both, as soon as possible. A preferable way would be to have a secretary present during the entire interview, wherein she made stenographic notes which were reduced to typewritten form as soon as possible. Her stenographic notes should be retained for evidenciary purposes.

2. Written Statements

A written statement may be as simple as: "Okay, Joe, you don't want to work here any more, then just give me a note of resignation for the file"; to something as complex as a multi-page court reporter's stenographic record of a question-and-answer confession, which would then be signed before witnesses and notarized.

The simple written statement is usually a basic narrative of fact or facts derived during the interview-interrogation: "I, John Doe, on this 32nd day of July, 1985, wish to resign my job for personal reasons, etc." This is a simple written statement, and if it is in the person's own handwriting, it would have evidenciary value even if it were unsigned. However, the addition of the signature would not change any basic facts but would merely lend greater weight to the statement.

The next form of written statement, which is more complex than the simple statement of fact, is the free-narrative written statement. The last form of written statement is the question-and-answer format.

There are a number of basic arguments for and against written statements that go beyond a basic statement of facts. A well-known federal prosecutor who was an acquaintance of one of the authors said, on numerous occasions: "I wish you hadn't taken so detailed a statement, because you may have limited me in the testimony that I can develop during the direct examination in court." This is, we suppose, the primary argument against the free-narrative and question-and-answer statements: that, in getting all the detail of the matter under investigation and reducing it to writing in the subject's handwriting, a limit may have been placed on later judicial inquiry.

Another argument against the complex written statement is that "No person in his right mind would furnish information so detailed, so complete, against his own interest."

Arguments for the complex written statement are that it provides the "very best evidence" at a given time as corroboration of what the person can testify to. A complex written statement, whether it be free-narrative or question-and-answer, has certain components, and whatever order these components fall into, they should be present in order to complete the prerequisites of judicial acceptance. The components of a complex statement are as follows:

    a. Title.

    b. Who is present.

    c. The date and beginning time.

    d. The location the statement is made at.

    e. Acknowledgement of rights.

    f. Waiver of rights.

    g. Knowledgeable waiver of rights.

    h. Material and relevant connection to the matter under investigation.

    i. Statement of the facts as developed during the interview/interrogation.

j. Collateral facts.

k. A further acknowledgement of voluntary quality and truth.

l. Signature.

m. Date.

n. Ending time of statement.

o. Witness (es') signature(s).

p. Identification of witness(es).

q. Date witness(es) signed statement.

r. Time witness(es) signed statement.

It is noted that swearing a statement before a notary may or may not increase the weight of the statement as the case occurs, but notarizing a written statement is just another form of witnessing the statement. We will go into reasons for notarizing a complex statement later in the chapter.

The free-narrative statement differs from the question-and-answer format in that everything is put on paper in the first person; i.e., "I did," "I saw," "I was," etc. The free-narrative has one advantage, and that is it severely limits any hearsay quality from getting into the statement. Bearing this in mind, free-narrative answers to the question-and-answer format are always desirable.

The main objection to the free-narrative statement is that after the statement has been admitted, provided it has all of the necessary components, should any one fact within that free narrative be shown as incompetent, then the entire statement could be impeached. The main advantage of the question-and-answer statement is that each question and answer is treated individually and that the interviewer/interrogator is merely making a record of actual testimony.

The interviewer/interrogator is making a record for possible later testimony. For example, he might be asked: "Did there come a time that you talked to this witness?" "Did there further come a time that you asked various questions of this witness?" "What were those questions?" and "How did the witness respond?"

The question-and-answer format has one disadvantage: It is somewhat unwieldy and quite formal in appearance, which could cause the witness or suspect to balk in giving it and later might cause the judicial body to become confused and to question that it is the "language" of the witness, although the questions are the language of the interviewer/interrogator and the answers are those of the subject. For this reason, the question-and-answer format should clearly label questions, statements, or remarks by the interviewer/interrogator; and separate by labeling from questions, remarks, or answers given by the witness.

We have found over the years that the best statement is a combination of question-and-answer and free-narrative, wherein many of the questions elicit free-narrative answers.

A further advantage that the question-and-answer statement has over the free-narrative is that the judicial acceptance of statements has become so complex that it is a valid argument in order to satisfy the requirements of a judicial body, the words in the free narrative are not those of the subject but, in fact, are dictated by the interviewer/interrogator, and this could lead to impeaching the entire statement. A question-and-answer statement written in the handwriting of the witness is most convincing, provided all questions and answers are clearly labeled. The optimum intaking of a question-and-answer statement is one wherein a stenographer is utilized and a stenographic record is kept along with the typewritten statement itself.

One method of easing the judicial requirements, overcoming the unwieldiness, and obtaining a uniform standard is through the introduction of a form which comprises the first eight (8) components of a statement. However, an argument against printed forms in the taking of statements is advanced by F. Lee Bailey and Henry B. Rothblatt in *Investigation and Preparation of Criminal Cases Federal and State,* the Lawyers' Cooperative Publishing Company, 1970, page 78, para. 129.

The printed form that we recommend, covering those first eight components, is a preamble to the actual statement, and the one-page preamble could be used by a stenographer for retyping as a formal statement. In fact, although it would seem redundant, we recommend that after such a preamble form is filled out by the witness, it should be retyped by the stenographer with the witness's answers typed in. A sample of the printed form is as follows:

DATE: _____

TIME: _____

MADE AT: _____

STATEMENT OF: _____

PRESENT ARE: _____

_____

Q: Do you speak, read, write, and comprehend the _____ language?

A: _____

_____, we represent _____ conducting an investigation for _____ of _____. Please be advised that I am about to ask you certain questions concerning _____. Also, please be advised that you cannot be forced to make any statement against yourself, that any statement you make either verbal or in writing can be used against you in a court of law as well as hearings, both public and private. Also, that you have the right to contact an attorney before proceeding further. Also, should this statement be used in a litigation or criminal proceeding, a court will provide legal counsel for you if you cannot afford same. Also, understand that any statement you make or give as a result of any threat, force, promises of reward or immunity would be invalid.

Q: Do you fully understand the above-mentioned rights?

A: _____

Q: Having these rights in mind, are you willing to make a statement at this time?

A: _____   (Signature)_____

Q: Before proceeding further with this statement; at the very outset of our meeting, did I inform you that I was not (if for police use, delete the word "not") a police officer, that you were not (if for police use, delete the word "not") under arrest, free to leave at any time (if for police use, delete words "free to leave at any time") and that you had a right to have a lawyer if you wanted one?

A: _____

Q: Do you wish a lawyer at this time?

A: _____

Q: Were you made any threats, abused in any way, or given any promises of any kind whatsoever?

A: _____

Q: Realizing that this statement could be used against you in a public hearing or court of law, why then are you willing to make it?

A: _____
       _____

Q: What is your full name, age, and home address?

A: _____

Q: What was the last grade in school that you completed and what school did you attend?

A: _____

Q: Where are you employed, for how long and what is your occupation?

A: _____

Q: Have you yourself (insert material and relevant connection to matter under investigation) _____?

A: _____

Q: Could you, in your own words, furnish a detailed narrative of events relative to these activities, through to the present time?

A: (Answer on next page)

This form has a great number of advantages, and we should like to note that in the very beginning of the form we have determined that the witness reads, writes, speaks, and comprehends the language of the statement. Thereafter, we have made the witness aware of his rights, and we ask for waiver of those rights. The insertion of the re-emphasizing paragraph, "Before proceeding further with this statement, at the very outset of our meeting . . . ," covers the hiatus in time between the beginning of the meeting between the interviewer/interrogator and the witness and the time that the statement was started. Thereafter, until that question, "Realizing that this statement could be used against you in a court of law, why then are you willing to make it?" all the preceding answers are "Yes" and "No" ones. However, this last question calls for a narrative type of answer which is "knowledgeable waiver" and, in effect, would be judicially interpreted the same as the question: "If you are foolish enough to make a statement against your own interest, what is your reasoning for this foolishness?"

The very last question in this preamble form elicits a narrative answer; and, in fact, the remainder of the statement may be taken totally in narrative form or the question-and-answer format may be utilized throughout, at the discretion of the interviewer/ interrogator. The one thing that we cannot supply is judgment; you will have to make up your own mind as to just which form (either question-and-answer or narrative) fits the given situation.

Whether a question-and-answer format or a free-narrative format is followed for the remaining body of the statement, it is advisable to deliberately insert one or two errors, either typographical or in the language of a question, on each page, which would then be corrected and initialed by the witness. This correction procedure corroborates the reading of the statement by the witness. However, the best method of having the voluntariness and acknowledgement of the statement proven is by having the witness read the statement aloud in the presence of witnesses, continuous motion pictures, and electronic recording equipment. Such evidence should be irrefutable.

When the statement is multi-paged, it is advisable for the subject, in his own handwriting, to put the time at the bottom of each page, together with either his initials or signature. If the statement is typewritten, then the time each page is completed should be typed at the bottom of each page.

Following the reading of the statement and the making of corrections, the witness should sign the statement in the presence of the interviewer/interrogator and witness(es).

As we stated previously, a notary is just another witness; however, the notary is usually disinterested, and this has great weight with a judicial body. Moreover, when a person raises his right hand and swears to a fact before a notary public, it would be very difficult to later recant that fact, saying "I deliberately lied," because they would then have committed the crime of false swearing, which in most cases is as serious a matter as perjury or the actual offense under investigation.

C. TESTING ASSERTIONS

Now that the statement has been taken, we will again, test all assertions.

We are put in mind of a classic case in Wisconsin where a man confessed to two murders and was later shown to have committed seven others. In more than fifty years of combined investigative experience, the authors have never been of the belief that a single written statement was completely factual or totally truthful the first time it was taken.

As we described earlier, in the intelligence community, it is standard practice to give cover stories to spies so that there was always a story within a story, and so it goes in life: there is always a story within a story within a story. If one thinks that criminal acts are complex, motivations toward those acts are even more complex.

We note that the basic methods used in testing assertions are:

1. Reinterview/reinterrogation (after a suitable time lapse).

2. Cross-checking.

3. Further investigation.

4. Polygraph verification (at an appropriate time).

5. Other psychological testing.

We should like to put into context the basic idea of testing assertions. As previously mentioned, there are a number of cases where the interviewer/interrogator is not primarily concerned with guilt or innocence, and the foregoing methods of testing assertions should only be considered as a guide in making such a judgment.

D. SAFEGUARDING

1. From Suspect/Subject

As each page of a statement is completed, put it in a safe place out of reach of the witness. All too frequently, witnesses will jump up after they have signed a statement that has been duly witnessed, grab the statement away, and have second thoughts about the whole matter, and may even destroy the written portion.

2. For Future Use

The statement may be the most valuable piece of evidence collected and should be kept under lock and key in an evidence file, even if it is a simple narrative of job resignation. For more complex criminal, or quasi-criminal proceedings, the statement should never be out of the custody of the interviewer/interrogator, so as not to "break" the chain of evidence.

13

PROOF OF LOSS
By Sanford E. Beck

13

PROOF OF LOSS
By Sanford E. Beck[*]

A. INTRODUCTION

The objective of any interview/interrogation is the gaining of usable intelligence. How you utilize that "intelligence," may win or lose for you in developing a proof of loss intended to produce maximum or optimum recovery on your crime insurance claim.

The law enforcement officer or security agent may gain sufficient intelligence in the matter to make an arrest that will culminate in a conviction; yet, recovery of lost assets is often the paramount consideration of the victim of the crime, the employer of the security agent, the client of the private investigator, the auditor, and/or the attorney involved. The "nitty gritty" of all this is that, in order to recover lost assets, intelligence obtained from an interview must be expanded upon and presented in a great number of ways. It must include information that the law-enforcement officer, security agent, or private-sector interviewer

---

[*]Sanford E. Beck. Vice President, Head of "Crime Loss" division, Management Safeguards, Inc.. Former Vice President in Charge, Fidelity Bond Claims for the country's oldest public adjusting firm. Former assistant to Chief Bonding Claims Attorney, Royal Globe Insurance Group. Staff member, Sobelsohn School of Insurance. Lectured on Crime Insurance at Pace College (N.Y.) and the College of Insurance. B.A. Economics, University of Rhode Island, L.L.B., Brooklyn Law School (N.Y.). Member of New York State Bar Association, New York Trial Lawyers Association, American Society for Industrial Security, National Association of Public Adjusters.

is seldom called upon to obtain. The police or private security interrogator will have to become familiar with requirements that go beyond the criminal law in order to obtain a greater degree of justice for the victim. Many times hearsay and other evidence usually inadmissible in criminal trials will, in fact, be admissible in the proof-of-loss negotiation.

B. OBJECTIVES

The interviewer has an obligation to make the reading of any statement as easy as possible. He must never forget what his underlying function is and must clearly understand the objectives of the ultimate reader of the written statement. In other words, the interviewer/interrogator must understand thoroughly the reason he is taking the statement and the ultimate use for which it is intended.

Written statements are used as evidence in a criminal or civil proceeding. The statements are also used in labor or union-related hearings and disputes, and they are utilized extensively in various administrative hearings and procedures. In addition, statements and confessions comprise a large body of writing in the area of insurance-related matters.

Of all these uses, statements and confessions used to support an insurance claim constitute one of the largest groups, if not the largest single group, of writings with which the interviewer/interrogator will be concerned. Insurance-related investigations, interviews, and statements—from automobile "fender-benders" to disability claims, from industrial accidents to confessions, from dishonest employees to conspiring managers—touch a great number of people each year.

C. DEVELOPMENT AND PREPARATION OF A CONFESSION SUPPORTING A FIDELITY INSURANCE CLAIM

The balance of this chapter will be devoted to the development and preparation of a confession for use in support of a fidelity insurance claim. The elements necessary to support a proof of loss, the claim document submitted by the insured in most insurance claims, will be covered. The depth of the interview outlined herein is more detailed than that necessary for the other types of insurance claims, but the basic concepts and factors touch upon all written statements, even those much narrower in scope.

Fidelity or bonding insurance covers almost 20% of the non-governmental work force in our country today. Private industry and certain governmental agencies bond their employees to reimburse the employer for dishonesty on the part of his employees. In the bonding concept, the employee is called "the principal"; the company, "the insured"; and the insurance carrier, "the surety."

The surety pays the insured for defaults or dishonesty on the part of the principal. The surety will pay for loss caused by dishonest employees occurring or discovered under the period of the bond. After payment of the loss to the insured, the surety is subrogated to the rights of recovery of its loss payment from the principal or others. In other words, if the insurer (the insurance company) has paid a loss as the result of dishonest acts on the part of an employee, it can pursue the employee and any others to attempt to recover its loss. That is the definition of term "subrogation."

Establishing Proof of Loss

Basic to the bond claim is the development of several factors for preparation of the proof of loss:

1. It must be proved that an employee breached his fiduciary capacity, or stole.

2. It must be proved that coverage for the act exists.

3. It must be proved that the loss was reported pursuant to policy provisions, which generally require reporting as soon as practicable after discovery of a dishonest act (this is to protect the subrogation rights of the surety).

4. The time when the first act of dishonesty occurred must be established.

5. The amount of loss, at cost or actual cash value, must be established.

6. A description must be provided of how the loss occurred and how it was discovered.

Let us consider the following problem and related factors: An employee working at a large manufacturing operation is apprehended as the result of surveillance by investigators. Apprehension occurs while he is removing a box of company product from a warehouse. The employee was observed placing the carton in his own vehicle. After the apprehension, he states that he has done this many times before and is willing to talk about it. Problem: To prove to the surety, by means of independent evidence, the theft and its related circumstances.

In this case, a statement or confession, coupled with the eyeball observation of the theft, is available. The amount of dollar loss can be sustained by the insured. We have been provided with the fact pattern that the employee admitted he had been stealing for a period of time; however, according to available statistics, inventory shortages are the major factor in establishing crime related losses in U.S. retailing and manufacturing today. The interrogation and subsequent confession will attempt to substantiate that a continuing long-term act of dishonesty, on the part of one or several employees, occurred. Thus is established the basic reason underlying the inventory shortage.

A statement to be used as evidence supporting dishonesty by employees should be a formal narrative of facts. The narration becomes the basis for the proof of loss. As a critical claim presentation document, a confession is a voluntary statement, made by one person to another, wherein the former acknowledges himself to be guilty of an offense. In the statement, he discloses the circumstances of the act or the share and participation he had in the activity.

The confession need not be spontaneously obtained, nor need it be made wholly at the maker's suggestion. It may be set in motion by external causes—in this situation, by an apprehension— so long as such influences are not what the law deems to be improper. Extra-judicial statements or confessions which are voluntary, along with supporting audit work to support the extent or amount of the insured's loss, are a good form of evidence in support of an insurance claim.

The statement or confession must be structured for *reasonableness, believability, and rationale,* as well as descriptive of methods and facts. In the example below, we will be taking a confession in support of a proof-of-loss form to be filed by the company (victim) for losses sustained by an employee's dishonest actions. The confession produces several factors necessary to support the insurance claim:

1. An admission of the act itself during the employment period, an explanation of the employee's duties and functions, and, if possible, an explanation of his ability to steal (including accessibility to stock and inventory).

2. A description of the time period of the theft and scope of the theft.

3. An exposition of how the stolen stock was disposed of and an explanation of the amount of payment received by the employee for the stolen goods, together with a revelation of what the subject did with the proceeds.

4. A confirmation of the scheme or conspiracy set forth in the confession.

Framing the Lead Question

I recommend the use of a question-and-answer format after the preliminary waiver and identification, as set forth in Chapter 12, is completed. The lead question, or first focus of attention, is crucial to setting the tempo of the confession.

The first question should "zero-in" precisely on the matters to be covered by the statement: "In this statement, John, we are going to review how, over the past 4½ years, you systematically stole merchandise from the company, causing it to suffer a financial loss. Do you understand?"

This type of lead sentence sets the stage for the interrogator and for the subject as well. You set up the procedure for the subject. The reason for the specificity of the statement is to develop the following:

1. The fact that the thefts spanned a long time period.

2. That the company was hurt and suffered financial loss which is all but in the words of the subject and stated in one short sentence.

The reader of the confession will also understand in the

beginning of the confession what direction to anticipate when he is reviewing the evidence which comes forth in the reading of the confession. The employee covered by an insurance policy has admitted stealing while he was employed by the insured. This opening gives rise to the insurance claim under the bond. The waiver and identification of the subject on the first page establish the other basics necessary for the establishment of the claim. The balance of the confession will provide the reader with the what, the where, the how, the why, and the balance of the "W's" referred to in Chapter 2.

Following the question sequences set forth earlier in this book, cover in the balance of the confession the why's and why not's. This reaching from the known to the unknown will help the reader understand the fraudulent methods employed by the subject and the difficulty or ease with which the acts of theft were accomplished.

What the Statement Must Establish to Substantiate Proof of Loss

We must consider the effect of the time period of the theft. The confession should establish:

1. Frequency.

2. The overall length of time involved.

3. Continuity.

4. Amount of theft on each occurrence.

5. The total number of units involved.

6. The total value of materials and money stolen.

I recommend reference to specific seasons in establishing frequency and in beginning coverage of the sequence of thefts. Question: "Did you steal when there was snow on the ground?" or "Did you steal when the air-conditioning was on in the plant?" Question: "Did you take a vacation last year?" This would be followed by "When?" You might add: "That means you worked for 50 weeks last year? Were you sick a few times? or were you out of work for other reasons?"

The problem which usually arises is the wrongful assumption that if John admits he stole $100 worth each week last year, his statement implies that his theft amounts to 52 x $100, or $5,200. In addition to John's two-week vacation, we may find that he took one full week off for a sprained leg, an additional week when his son got in trouble, and that he was on temporary lay-off for two weeks when there was a labor dispute several months before. In reality, John was only employed full-time for 46 weeks; therefore, if we are going to believe his statement, he could only have stolen $4,600. *An erroneous computation undermines the entire statement and its believability.*

Concerning the length of time covered by the theft, John may say: "I started to steal a few years ago." The questioning should then narrow his statement down to a year, a month, a season, a week, a day, or to any specific time span, by reference to dates of employment or other pertinent dates. "Did you steal soon after you started working?" "Was it during the winter?" "Do you remember the first thing you stole?" "How did you do it?" "How did you get it out of the building?"

The first step in a continuing series of episodes is usually memorable to the subject. His recollection must be refreshed by the interviewer/interrogator, however.

Regarding continuity, you might pose the questions: "Did you continue to steal regularly since then?" "That means for the past 4½ years you have been taking out merchandise, is that correct?" "Was there any time you were able to take out more than you were at other times?" "When?" "Why?" "Did your thefts continue?" "What happened when you were sick or on vacation?"

To compile the total amount of theft attributable to this subject, it is necessary to probe into the amount stolen each time. Once the frequency and length of time have been established, you must establish with the same systematic approach the questions regarding how much was stolen each time: "How much (or "How many) did you take each time when you first started?" "Did the amount you were able to take increase?" "When?" "What was the most you were able to take at one time?" "When?" "How?" "How heavy would ten boxes be?" "How big are the boxes (or containers)?" "How did you fit them into your lunch pail (or pockets)?" "What type of car do you own?" "Did you ever use a station wagon or truck?" "When?" "How many times?" "How much could the truck hold?"

After this line of questioning, attempt to conclude the total amount stolen by summarizing the total number of times, the length of time, the amount each time. Expand the figures into total units; develop total prices from the value of each unit. The interviewer/interrogator should use a separate sheet of paper specifically constructed to corrolate with the statement by date, time, name of investigation, etc. Ask the subject to write the numbers in his own handwriting, where practicable, or to validate, with his signature or initials, the interviewer's handwritten interpretation. If an adding machine tape is being used, the subject may be asked to follow the same procedure. In both instances, the subject should be requested to date his entries. This may be done by reference if tape recording or transcription is utilized.

The idea is to establish the number of units taken during each unit of time—a day, a week, etc.—and multiplying that figure by the number of these time units contained in the overall time period being examined. The record sheets should be large enough for the calculations necessary and should provide space for totals encompassing the number of units in the entire time period. Of course, the same procedure would be followed for theft of cash.

Sample Interrogatories That Establish Recoverable Value

Let us consider the subject of value. As indicated earlier in this chapter, most insurance coverage is written at actual cash value: this means at the cost to the insured, of the company, not its resale, retail, or wholesale level. It is essential that the interviewer/interrogator have some idea as to the average cost of the employer's product. This knowledge can be gained through price lists, catalogs, pictures of the type of merchandise, etc. The interviewer must have these in his possession prior to the interview/interrogation, so that the transition from the total number of units to the total value can be accomplished in terms of dollars.

In instances where a variety of products and numerous price ranges are involved, a weighted average cost must be determined before the interrogation: "John, we see that, based on the number of months we have just put on this summary sheet, and which you identified, you took 2,500 units over this 4½ year period of time. Do you have any idea how much each item cost the company? Here's a copy of the price list with the items you've been telling me about. It's dated 1/31/?, and it tells me that the value is $10 at cost for each unit. Let's complete that summary sheet now, by multiplying the 2,500 units that you've admitted taking by $10 each, okay? How much is that? That is $25,000, correct? Do you see how we arrived at that figure? Correct? Excuse me, do you see how we arrived at that figure? Could you initial the $25,000 number?"

What has been accomplished in the preceding example is a systematic, realistic computation by the subject, with guidance from the interviewer, to a logical, believable conclusion. To prove this number, however, in the mind of the reader and to convince the subject that over this long period of time the small items he took each week cost the company thousands of dollars, further confirmation is needed.

With reference to the disposal of stolen stock, consider what the subject, or employee, has done with the property. What about his share of the proceeds? Interviewers seem to "slack off" when the logical pattern of the statement leads to this matter. To make the statement credible, a thorough discussion of this aspect of the act is of great importance.

You might find useful the questions: "John, you just told me that you got the stuff home in your car and then sold it. Could you tell me to whom?" "How often did you sell it?" "What did you sell it for?" "What was the largest amount you ever sold?" "Who else did you sell it to?" "Did they pick it up? or did you deliver it to them?" Such a line of questioning, at this point, can get much more than a mere ascertainment of the dollar value to the thief. "What was the largest amount you ever got for selling?" "In other words, you averaged about 50¢ on the dollar—is that what you're telling me?" "Then you got about $12,500 over this period of time, is that right?" "What did you do with the money?" "What did you buy?" "What bills did you pay off?" "What debts did you pay?"

At this juncture, you can get into the questions of alcohol, gambling, stock market, and loans, and might ask specific questions about how much money the subject has in the bank and what bank, how much of it goes into his car and clothing, etc. "At a girlfriend's house?" "Have you taken any vacations?" "Were there any serious illnesses in the family?" "Did you take any extensive travel?" "Did you pay any debts to friends or relatives?" "Do you have any problems with your parents? Your children?" Only if these questions are asked in this probe at a level more personal than we have before examined do we pick up the answers which lead to credibility and conclusion of realism in the statement taken.

The subject has now left his job environment and has admitted to stealing in it. He enters his private, protected world, disposing of the bounty. Exploration of this area not only supports the credibility of the entire confession, but may provide the interviewer with the rationale behind the thefts. In most cases, such rationale is logical: "I saw an opportunity to make easy money."

In addition, an insurance-related concept being kept in mind is the subrogation rights of the insurer, or the rights of the insurance company to be reimbursed, or subrogated, for losses it pays as a result of the dishonesty of a principle who stole or from any other owner who did not pay the proper consideration for it. The interviews in this area will frequently disclose an asset, purchased with the proceeds of this theft even if only for a small amount.

Methods of Documenting a Long
Term Theft Situation

Another question arises in the course of an interrogation wherein an employee has confessed to thefts spanning a period of more than ten or even twenty years: How do we best reduce this to writing so as to provide credibility to the reader? That is the question; the answer is: For a time period which would be beyond the scope of normal memory or normal recollection, use a shorter time period as a point of reference. For instance, a three-year time period—3 years back from the date of confession or even 5 years—is acceptable and within the realm of possibility to the subject. Then, after summarizing what has occurred for the last 5 years, specifically ask questions about: "Would you say, within the last 10 years preceding this period of time prior to 1970 that your dishonest activities cost the company more than they did in this 5-year period of time?" "And, if you were stealing 15 years before that, would you say that within that 5-year period of time it's the same thing?"

In other words, working backwards in segments, you got him to admit that in the last 5 years he stole $6,000. He admitted that in the last 4½ years he stole $5,000 worth of merchandise and, in fact, he has been employed by the company for 10 years. Just ask him the question: "Did you steal the same amount in the 5 years prior to 1970?"

This question has been asked, "Would that stand up in an insurance claim?" I do not know specifically if it would stand up as a valid claim against the surety for thefts or disappearance of merchandise in that time period, but it would be of some significance to the bonding company. This is because one of the bonding concepts, which I am not detailing at this point, is that if an insured company has had fidelity bond coverage for 20 years, even though it was with 9 different insurance companies for this period time, the following situation prevails: As long as there was continuous coverage without a lapse, the last, or current, insurance company is responsible for losses going back that full 20 years of time, as if it had issued coverage from 1956 to 1976. That is called "superseded suretyship." Even though the back coverage, going back to the 1950's and 1960's, was held by another company, as long as there was continuous bond coverage held on this employee the current insurance carrier will pick up the entire loss.

This is, therefore, a very peculiar form of insurance. Your basic fire insurance policy, or automobile policy, or compensation policy pays coverage only within its time period. *The fidelity bond carrier, however, will pay losses for as far back as there was continuous coverage.*

Let's pick up from that time on and suppose the subject says: "Okay, I've been doing it for the last ten years." He might give explicit situations for the last five years. He continues: "Yes, it's been happening at least ten years. The interviewer/interrogator comments: "(So much) per week?" and the subject comes back: "Yes, yes, and three times a day," and tells how he has been removing the merchandise. Often, when you are dealing with a statement such as that and you do your multiplication, coming up with let us say $85,000 over the last ten years, the subject "turns off" completely. He possibly says; "It couldn't have been that much," this despite the fact he is agreeing with you up to "Yes, (so much) per week; yes, (so much) per time, "this is how I've been doing it." When he sees that "blockbuster," though, he recants the whole thing.

Now, for an insurance situation, that is it! Although the statement is good to have, that is the situation. If the subject is explaining that he removed so much per day, at the end of the statement it can be multiplied out. When you are determining how much was taken, the subject may think, "Must he put that big number in?" and must you say, "Gee, that's a large number! Are you sure you stole that much?" Need you do that?

At some point in time near the end of the written confession, the professional interrogator may reach a point where he feels that if he probes too deeply into a particular area he will lose control of the subject. He fears that he may not get his subject ultimately to agree to everything that was previously stated. Yet, acknowledgment of the big number in his statement is most advantageous.

The novice may continue by reflecting: "Well, yes, when he sees that large number it 'turns him off.' He says, 'Well, no, it couldn't have been that many thousands of dollars over that time period. It couldn't have been. I must be wrong'."

My solution is basic. You must push and probe as in any other aspect of this interview to the extent you can do so. Then, the professional interrogator must make a decision as to whether or not he is going to probe and push to the limit. The limit here is in terms of the amount, the number of years, the personal relationships involved, and in terms of implications of conspiracy with other employees. Sometimes you do reach a particular cut-off point.

The interrogator, in this instance, might proceed by saying: "What I am saying, Harold, is $6,000 appears to be a lot of money." Suppose that after the interrogator repeats this phrase the subject then realizes that the interrogator is talking about $6,000. Sometimes the interviewer/interrogator cannot get away with it. It might become a "tug-of-war" if you were to confront the subject with: "Gee, Harold, your number indicates that over the last five years you've stolen $82,000 worth of product." The subject is likely to say, "No way!" Here we have "the straw that broke the camel's back." The interrogator must feel the attitude of the subject and know how far the subject will go.

The solution is set forth in the pertinent chapters of this book. We know that the psychology which motivates the subject and the psychology which motivates the interviewer must be kept in bounds at all times. I would advise that when you get to a point where you believe you have pushed the questioning beyond a certain limit—in terms of dollars, in terms of time, etc.—you accept the fact that you have a decision to make. You must cut short the time period, cut short the dollars, etc. Essentially, what you want is the optimum possible.

The less experienced interviewer might say: "You're missing my point. He already went the time period. Must I have a question with that big number in it?" In other words, does the subject have to make that computation? Will the insurance company honor the claim if it just has so much per day, so much per unit, and so much of a time period? Must the interrogator put in: "Gee, Harold, that amounts to $82,000?"

I do not feel that you have to put in the big number if you feel it is going to prejudice the end results; namely, a total and full voluntary confession. You are not entrapping the subject; you are not violating any particular statutes or case law, in that you are not taking it out of the realm of a voluntary confession. Again, however, the judgment of the interviewer in this regard—as to naming the specific total dollar amount above and beyond a short time period—must be made on the basis of whether such inclusions would cause loss of control of the subject. If these inclusions would have such an adverse effect, they should be waived and the next topic should be opened.

In interrogation and the taking of a signed statement, under optimum conditions the subject should furnish a complete and totally voluntary confession. Ideally, there are no other time pressures, no further investigative work necessary, no other intervening or confusing side facets, no time limits, and no limit on cooperation from the subject. I believe that we can strive for maintenance of high standards and that a systematic approach to these interviews in order to get the most mileage from them.

TAILOR THE STATEMENT TO MEET YOUR OBJECTIVE

In many interrogations, the time factor is the real enemy. No matter how many people we have to interview/interrogate or what the circumstances are, we're always dealing with the time factor in obtaining sufficient information from the subject before he gets to the point where he jsut says "No." Sometimes you do not have any breakthrough. The subject admits only to what you have already learned. How do you take a statement that will cover his admissions and yet meet some of the objectives?

The time span is directly related to the particular subject. In certain situations where the time span is short, you have to sacrifice some of the specific details you are looking for in an insurance statement. This is so because in your judgment you feel you are going to lose control of the subject. Before you walk into the location of the interrogation, you should have determined the needs and objectives of your client. If your sole objective is to remove the employee from the work environment due to any reason, then you approach the time element to obtain sufficient information and a statement to meet your limited objective. If your objective is to assist in a later situation—for unemployment insurance purposes, quasi-legislative, or administrative hearings—extreme detail is superfluous and really not necessary. What I am basically discussing is a specific statement being prepared as a confession for a specific objective, namely, to collect money from an insurance company because the employee who stole was bonded. The interviewer must determine that objective before he goes into the interviewing room.

Persons and Acts Coverable by the Bond

Many times we are questioning truck drivers, janitorial workers, or sales personnel who we believe are employed by the client firm, and we learn that they are outside contractors or freelance operators who are paid per diem or by the hour. Technically, they would not be covered by the fidelity bond.

An employee has been defined as any worker who on a regular basis is paid by the company and for whose services payments are written, withholding taxes collected, social security or other health benefits are withheld, or for whom the company exercises the right and privilege to hire or fire. This is a rough definition of an employee who would be covered under a fidelity bond.

How would you classify an outsider, contracted for but who receives a regular pay check? He does not have taxes out of his pay, though he could be hired or fired and he is covered by the client's health and insurance program. In my opinion, this outside contractor would be an employee under the client's fidelity bond.

Although he is an outside contractor he is sufficiently within the client's control. His access to the client's operation, their files, and their assets is such that, even though some of the types of normal exercise an employer has over an employee are missing, there are many others which do exist. I would deem him to be an employee of the firm, covered under the bond.

In American industry today, there are two basic forms of fidelity bond coverage:

1. The blanket fidelity bond, which gives coverage to all employees in various categories as long as they work for the parent company, or insured. The policy usually establishes a specific limit either on total dollar losses due to an employee or others working in conspiracy, or it states specific limits for each employee. It does not, however, break down by name the particular employees.

2. The specific fidelity bond, which is the type of insurance prevalent in American industry today. It names specific employees, with their titles or job functions. It sets a particular limit under the bond for which the bonding company, or surety, will be responsible.

What about the employee who does not steal from the company but purposely, and on many occasions over the years, damages the equipment or machinery on which he is working. To paraphrase it: If an employee damages or sabotages the company property or merchandise but does not steal it, would coverage be available? Under a form of fidelity bonding coveraged called "3D", the answer is "Yes." That coverage includes disappearance, destruction, and damage.

Under certain other forms of crime insurance coverage now

being broadly sold, only fraudulent acts or acts of larcenists are covered. The answer to the above mentioned question is, therefore, both "Yes" and "No," depending upon the type of coverage.

Making an Accusation

Primarily, the establishment of proof-of-loss includes the naming of an employee as being dishonest, setting forth some of the employment history and background, and identifying the time period within which he worked. There must be a specific allegation made by the client that the man is a thief and that he has stolen.

That particular type of statement in the proof-of-loss form is tantamount to libel and slander and can give rise to law suits by the employee. Frequently the questions are posed: Do we have enough information to name this man as a thief? Are we liable? May we be subject to a libel action? If we choose to prosecute, could false imprisonment and false prosecution charges be made against the client? Various types of civil actions could be raised by an employee against his employer.

These determinations must be set forth in the proof of loss. The publication or naming of the employee on the proof-of-loss form becomes libel per se, inasmuch as that document is published, essentially, to the world and holds the employee up to ridicule in his business community, in his profession, and in his environment. That is a description of what a libel action is.

A slander action is the same thing done orally. A libel is the accusation in a written form. False imprisonment and false arrest similarly arise if prosecution follows.

Confirmation of Statement's Validity

One of the most important concepts in understanding the language of a fidelity bond is that the surety reserves no rights, nor does it pose any requirement upon the insured, to prosecute. There is no mention in the language of the policy that the acts of a dishonest employee must be reported to the police or to law-enforcement agencies. There is no language in the standard form of fidelity policy that requires prosecution. We are looking for prosecution:

1. To confirm the investigative results.

2. To confirm and finalize the confession.

3. To verify the amount, the time, the value, and the disposal of stolen property.

4. To confirm the confession as to how the thefts continued without detection.

5. To probe the possibility of co-conspirators.

6. To understand how this employee could have accomplished the feat he has confessed to, within the time period, without being detected. (This becomes, for the reader, a matter of believability.)

At this point, we have established the average cost per unit, the number of individual thefts, and the total value of the loss. We established the total value of thefts to the subject, in terms of his "take," and the extent of the time period in question.

Confirmation by another measurement is necessary. In this confirmation phase, it is not unusual to discover that either the time, the amount, or the frequency has been understated because of the subject's response to the kind of questioning. Since the subject has acknowledged gross amount of loss in units, dollars, and time, a responsible interviewer/interrogator must test theory: "John, I would like to review what we have gone over so far. How big were the boxes you took? Were they bigger than this radio?" By the principle of association or by reference to the size, the subject can recall how big, how many, and how much.

Questioning regarding specifics of the process of secreting, transporting, and selling are usually developed. The exposure of methods employed in removing the stock adds realism to the figures earlier given relating to the amount of loss in dollars: "John, you were able to get out six cartons each week, is that right? What was the largest number of cartons you got out at one time? Did you have help? Who? How did you do it without getting caught? Did you ever fear getting caught? Did anyone ever see you taking stock out?" These last questions can possibly, even if the subject has denied participation by others, open up the possibility of witnesses who may have seen the theft taking place but were not co-conspirators.

Attempt to ascertain if any of the stolen property is around and available. Arrange to get it back—from friends, from family, from third party distributors, or from a fence. Not only does recovery, even a small amount, tend to confirm what has been given in the confession, but it may lead to other areas of investigation and subsequent confirmation by others as to frequency and amount of stock handled by the subject.

Tape recording of the entire interview is an effective confirmation of the validity, the sincerity, and the voluntariness of the subject's responses. Written statement form is acceptable, but where practicable tape recording and video taping is desirable. Photographs of the subject, his home, his car, and stolen property which has been recovered, or returned, add to credibility.

Verification by polygraph (lie detector) as to extent and time period confessed can add immeasurably to the confimation of the statement made by the subject. Confirmation of "cut," or share, of proceeds of the theft by means of this method of polygraph can open new areas for further interviewing. If test results reveal that answers are not truthful, specific probes by additional questioning, before the statement is concluded, can effectively determine more detailed information.

Confirming the memory of witnesses of other facts about weather, political activities, or other specific events which happened two or three years ago will reinforce the subject's recall of dates and timing in the confession: "John, what you have told me indicates a lot of this occurred during the Vietnam War period, is that right? Do you remember stealing while Eisenhower was in the White House?" Some of these questions, although seemingly of no great value, have great impact on the reader and provide a frame of reference—or, in some instances, establish a long time period of theft.

The principal should be made aware of the fact that the insured had coverage for loss incurred because of his activity. This awareness should appear in his confession. He should be informed, on record, that what he is saying can be used against him, not only in judicial proceedings (as done on the initial page) but also in civil action brought by the employer or by the surety. The subject should be told that he, even if financially incapable at the moment, has an obligation to repay this money.

Where evidence has been accumulated during investigation or provided by the subject, identification of items that enhance the statement should be included in the body of the confession: "John, do you recognize this box?" Answer: "Yes, this is the type I was taking merchandise out in." Interrogator: "This box, which we will call Exhibit 1B1, was taken from your car, is that correct?" Answer: "Yes." Interrogator: "Would you please identify this by placing your initials here?" Answer: "Okay." Interrogator: "Is this the size of the box you were referring to?" Answer: "Yes." Interrogator: "Is this the general size of box you were stealing with at the rate of six a day?" If documents are evidence, specific reference to them—explicit explanations of how they apply to confirmed portions of the confession—can be helpful. Identification of photographs, of catalogs, and of brochures listing items stolen can answer many of the ultimate questions of the reader about amount, description, size, and value.

Intentional errors in typing or handwriting, which require correction by the subject in his handwriting, add to the credibility of the language contained in the body of the confession and point up the fact that the subject was fully aware of the nature of his acts. By his manually making corrections, it is established that he has reread, rephrased, or looked at specific pages of the confession. It ultimately adds an aura of voluntariness and understanding on the part of the subject.

Finally, witnessing by the interviewer and others indicates the elapsed time of the interview, the date of the interview, and the date of the transcription, where applicable. This is a must. Use of a notary public, for secondary confirmation, is of no great importance in insurance claims, but conceivably it can add more credibility and support to the fact that the witness' signature is to a document which he understands to be a confession and that it is voluntary.

I recommend that statements be free narrative in form and that they be in the handwriting of the subject; the reason is basic credibility. A reader understands that this is the handwriting of the subject; he knows that nobody else was holding the pen, and he understands with greater feeling that if the subject was doing this in his own handwriting, it is more valid.

As a practical matter, the question-and-answer statement format, written in the handwriting of the subject, may be more desirable than the free narrative form. I believe that a combination of both is the most practical form.

A lead suggestion calling for a long narrative answer on the part of the subject can probably accomplish both of these: "John, I want you, in your own words, to describe how you did this." Then allow John to describe, in his own words, how he took the merchandise out. Do not allow him to ramble, however, and to go into many other areas: "Now, in your own words, can you tell me how you disposed of the merchandise?" Allow the free narrative to flow.

In many confessions and statements, unfortunately, the questions are considerably longer than the answers. This detracts from credibility in the eyes of an outside but involved reader.

Obviously, however, a long, rambling answer has other perils. In many instances, the subject gets lost. He can cross into other areas.

Covering motive, intent, method, and amount can take a greater length of time. It is up to the interviewer, who has to be extremely proficient, to cut off the free narrative when it gets too far from the objective. This becomes increasingly difficult when the free narrative is being written by the subject.

To repeat, the most practical form appears to be free narrative, with both questions and answers written by the subject.

Establishing a Basis for Recovery in the Case of Outside Co-conspirators

With regard to co-conspirators you have to comprehend basic penal law definition. Here is a case history to illustrate.

"XYZ" Candy Company is a very religious, kosher operation. Because of that fact, only devout Hasidic Jews handle the candy. In order to get their work force started on a 7:30 a.m. production schedule, the company allows these employees to pray every morning, as they must do to observe their concepts, in a special temple within the "XYZ" candy factory. Also because of their religious beliefs, on certain days Hasidic Jews cannot turn on electric lights or turn off electric machinery.

In order to make these observances possible, a non-Jewish janitor was hired. His main function was to open the door, allow these religious men in, usher them into their synagogue in the morning, close the door, and start up the production facility. The janitor also had to await the arrival of the balance of the packing employees, who did not have to be zealously religious, and shipping employees who did not touch the candy.

The janitor merely opened a back door every morning at 6:45 a.m., when everybody was inside praying, and he came back and closed the door at 7:59 a.m. prior to the employees' going in. For these duties, he received $60 or $70 a week over a year and a half time period.

What was really going on during this period in the open factory? A team of eight or ten men came into the building, loaded trucks and pallets of candy onto a vehicle outside the door, and removed about $700,000 worth of candy in less than one year. All thieves were nonemployee truck drivers, and this theft occurred during working hours while thirty-five of forty other employees were on the premises. Although the janitor received nothing for his activity, or inactivity if you will, he too was on the premises; he was, in fact, doing a favor for a friend.

The janitor was an employee, however, and for his participation in the crime he was, in the eyes of the law, an equal co-conspirator. Without his participation in this crime, a fidelity claim was impossible. Except for his participation, however, there would not have been a loss—because access to the building could not have been had if he had not left the door open and bypassed the alarm circuitry. This case was settled for the policy limit of $500,000.

Let us take a hypothetical case. An interrogator interviews 15 employees, and 4 say: "Yes, I stole. I stole in collusion with John Jones"; "Yes, I stole not only for myself, I also helped steal with John Jones," etc. You have 4 employees relating the same story, so you talk to John Jones—and he "doesn't know what you are talking about."

Now, if you have that many people who were not in collusion together, but were colluding individually with John Jones, saying, "Yes, I stole with John Jones," can you include this information in the claim? Bear in mind, you do not have the statement from John Jones.

In my opinion, the answer is "Yes." You have to answer whether or not a fidelity bond insures as it basically exists. You can name an employee whom you believe to be dishonest but who has not confessed; it is done every day in the week. The insured has a decision to make, however: Do they dare name this man as a thief predicated on the statement of others who are admitted co-conspirators and theives themselves? That is a policy-making decision the insured has to make.

The standard fidelity bond form must have a provision by which unnamed employees can be claimed as if they were one single employee; then a separate proof-of-loss can be filed specifically naming "an individual."

Let's consider another possible case. There is a series of confessions related to how certain people disposed of great quantities of merchandise, thousands of units—you have that in writing by several people. Yet, you have not confirmed any of these sales to outside peddlers, or fences, at this point because the client has a limited budget. He cannot afford to investigate these actions further and in detail. Can the insured afford to confirm the facts of various conspiracies evident through statements? If you are talking about a business decision, can he afford not to do so?

That is a decision the insured must make, because the insurance company does not pay for the investigation. Sometimes, in fact, the insurance company does not pay for the in-depth and extremely expensive audit which has to be performed, nor does it pay for surveillance. It will not pay for any of these things, because the primary burden of proof is upon the insured: he must prove to the surety what the principal has done, for how long he has done it, and how much he has done.

Suppose you are in that situation and you feel that the additional investigation is necessary. The client then raises the question of cost, which let us presume is $10,000. How badly off is the client? What will be the consequences if he does not authorize further investigation? After all, the thieves were not employees of his company; suppose he does not authorize you to continue. How badly does that jeopardize the claim? The answer is that every situation is different.

I am aware of a large statement in which two subjects jointly indicated they had sold stolen merchandise to barber shops, and that the value of the goods was in the vicinity of $80,000. The insurance company, at this point, specifically stated they did not believe that this occurred. They did not feel that, through the channels described, the subjects could have sold 16,000 units at $4 or $5 a unit.

The client had a money decision to make in considering further investigation. If he authorized additional inquiry, would he get more dollars in insurance recovery? He could not be guaranteed anything in that respect. Here the cost of the investigation becomes a major factor and may determine whether or not there will be an investigation.

Suppose we assume the client has authorized continued investigation. For purposes of confirmation, you attempt to interview a third party, a fence, and he says: "Get out of my store." Such a failure on your part should not jeopardize the investigation. Even that hostile, negative attitude of the fence is proof of something; to some degree it might influence a more favorable claim settlement.

Addenda to the Statement

There are problems with addenda.

In the practical use of addenda, or add-ons, with reference to an original statement, they are, for the most part, disbelieved by the insurance company regarding the honoring of an insurance claim. If it is at all possible, include everything in the first statement. For example, take the confession dated on a February 20 that runs 9 pages. Rather than add an addendum to it, rewrite the 9 pages, date it later, and encompass the additional material by making it a longer confession. The only change is the addition of pages.

The interviewer/interrogator should specifically identify what he is going after: "John, these are the other co-conspirators." If you do not want to use that language, you might try: "These are the other cats that you took with, right?" Let us presume the subject answers, "Yes." You add: "What were their names?" Subject possibly replies: "John, Joe, and Frank." You query: "Are there any others?" Subject could reply, "No." You follow with: "If you think of any others, let me know before we finish this tape recording."

Should an interrogation be recorded in its entirety? A sound guideline is record all interviews and interrogations. As a guide for the interrogator, not necessarily as evidence or proof to be submitted to anybody else, it can be the solution to many problems.

An interrogator, sometimes goes to the extreme of pretending to be somebody he is not—such as an insurance adjustor. This in itself could ruin a claim.

When you are in a major situation and a subject is giving you a statement of more than $20,000, my suggestion is: Tape record everything. The ultimate use of the tape is a matter for future consideration, but it should be available. To repeat, I recommend that major interviews/interrogations be taped. *(Regarding taping, state laws regulate the practice and/or its clandestine use.)*

An insurance company claims manager has said that video tape allows him to see and hear the subject in the process of making a statement and that this resulted in increased compensation to the insured. The statement was made more believable.

Duty to Repay

Somewhere in the statement the subject should indicate in writing that he knows he may have to repay the insurance company. Understandably, the interrogator would not want to stress this. The insurance company would want it, but one of the interviewer's wedges is to say: "Okay, you stole many thousands of dollars, all of which we're going to claim from the insurance company."

I will not yield on this point, however. The subject realizes that what he said may be used against him. He realizes that he might have to pay his due by serving time in jail and that he may lose his job. The subject is not reserving any rights in these matters, nor are we waiving any. Everybody who steals thinks he is doing it for basic reasons. Essentially, he is going to own up to it, though, and have to pay for it in one way or another. The fact that a man serves a jail sentence has nothing to do with the fact that he may be civily liable for stealing the merchandise or the money or that he has to pay it back.

Here I would like to make an exception to the rule about not taking addenda. I suggest that the interviewer take an addendum or an additional statement to cover the financial approach, and that this follows the original statement. This, in my opinion, is a practical approach.

It is the obligation of the insured, in submitting a fidelity bond claim, to make an accusation. He has to make a statement and support it with an audit. The insurance company, after this burden of proof has been assumed by the insured, does things also:

1. They re-audit the figures.

2. They recheck the coverage to see if the subject is an employee.

3. They check the period during which he worked to verify that it is within the framework of the policy.

4. They go out to this employee and ask him if this is his statement.

Is there any attempt on the part of the insurance company, during the re-interview of the subject, to try to obtain another statement attacking the original? Absolutely! Remember, we are talking about the magic phraseology, "extra-judicial investigation"—outside of the courtroom. They are in the man's home, he is relaxed, his children are running around, etc. He has a beard. Either he has been arrested, or he has not been arrested.

They walk in and they say: "John, see this statement. In it, you admit stealing $25,000 from your company, is that true?" You may envision that he is not being interrogated on company premises, or in a sophisticated investigative environment, or in a motel room. It is several months later, or several weeks later. He has had a chance to think about what he did, and the trained investigator from the insurance company is out to get basic facts—just as you are. He is trying to get believable facts.

The insurance investigator will take that statement, chapter and verse: "When did it occur? What room was it? Was it 8:00 in the morning? Was it 10:00 p.m.?" That is where you get the total mark. I am not talking about a secondary interview: "John, I have this piece of paper which you separately listed." The subject says: "That's not my handwriting, I didn't write that." "Well," says the investigator, "Who wrote that?" John replies: "Oh, that was the interviewer." Investigator: "Is that your name on it?" John says:

"Sure, he told me to sign it." Investigator: "Did you read it first?" John: "I don't remember, I'd sign anything. I just wanted to get out of that room." Investigator: "So, in other words, you're saying that those numbers on that piece of paper really don't mean anything?" John: "Oh, no, that's crazy! I didn't steal $150 a week. I meant $150 a month. It's just a simple misunderstanding. I stole, but I only took $150 a month, not a week." The insurance company investigator will sit down and, as lengthy as the statement is, explain the whole story at $150 a month, not at $150 a week.

Now comes the big measurement: Where does the credibility lie? Who is telling the truth? Is it John, the employee, who is under tremendous pressure and who has just been apprehended? or is it John sitting in his undershirt and shorts in his home drinking a beer and talking to an insurance investigator? The latter is saying: "You have to pay that money."

This is why I say the matter of understanding duty to repay amounts stolen should be covered in the confession—if possible, 100% of the time. Let the subject know that someone is going to come around and test him: "Mister, let's make it clear that you know this statement is going to be used against you some time and that this is your voluntary statement." Then you have in reality two statements.

A simple form could be used for insurance claim purposes: "I, John Doe, have signed the confession which was 9 pages and witnessed by Joe Jones. I further understand that this statement was voluntary and that at some later date I may have to review this question with representatives of an insurance company. I still maintain that it is truthful and factual, and I further understand that I was bonded, like hundreds of other employees of this firm. I further understand that because I stole I will have to reimburse or pay back, in any way I can possibly do it, the insurance company."

A bonding company will pursue thieves where there is a chance of recovery, and will do so for many years. That is the reason why the client company has a fidelity bond insurance policy. The client could sue John Jones and get a civil judgment against him for perhaps $25,000. The judge might say to the subject: "All right, you have to pay it back at $1,000 a year for twenty-five years."

The company could respond: "We do not want to wait twenty-five years for our money; we want it now." The insurance company (surety) company does wait, however. Of course, it pays the loss immediately, and then proceeds, by using its subrogation rights, to collect $1,000 a year for twenty-five years. I know of one case in which an employee has been making reimbursement payments since 1947, and there are hundreds of thousands of employees who are paying back fidelity claims this way.

Sometimes it is also possible to have investigators visit the subject's home. Immediate questioning may reveal that certain electrical appliances, vehicles, etc., are in fact fruits of his theft. Upon admission this is so, by the subject, he may agree to confiscation and authorize it with a release. Subject may admit that a bank account is the result of his theft; a cashier's check for total withdrawal may help compensate the insurance company and serve as further validation of the confession. The more evidence you can obtain—in terms of cashiers' checks, confiscated property, etc.—the more believable is the statement.

14

ETHICS AND STANDARDS

14

ETHICS AND STANDARDS

A. ATTITUDE

Without saying that "The end justifies the means," we can certainly postulate that results are the test of right and wrong. Working from this premise, we note that most interviewer/interrogator results usually are directly proportional to the initial attitude of the interviewer or interrogator prior to his meeting with the witness, suspect, or subject.

We are not critical of law-enforcement interrogators, having both been in the enforcement field at the outset of our careers, but we wish to note that there is total polarity among most enforcement interrogators. That is to say, by and large among enforcement interrogators, they are either great or they are poor. This has nothing to do with training, but rather is an extension of their awareness of themselves and the attitudes which may be restricting to interrogation that are engendered by the enforcement field itself.

The enforcement officer, by the nature of his job, sees himself as an extension of legally constituted authority (and this is as it should be). This situation leads, however, to the attitude and judgment that the most serious crime that can be committed is resisting authority (resisting questioning, resisting arrest, resisting interviewing, resisting interrogation, etc.), which in many cases causes the idea that resistance or dissent in any form is criminal (and this is not as it should be, for our very national heritage was born out of dissent).

When earlier we referred to a submissive attitude, we were talking about psychological submissiveness, for it is completely natural that any human would wish to preserve his privacy, his civil rights, and his liberty. It is natural that a person committing a criminal act does not wish to discuss it. It is natural that a witness does not wish to be involved, and only by presenting alternative routes can we change the direction of this witness, suspect, or subject who has taken a natural defensive structure.

We cannot present these alternatives if we are not aware of the existing attitudes in ourselves and in the witnesses, suspects, subjects. This cycle of awareness starts with us, for we are the controllers of the situation. If we were not, we would be answering questions and giving statements. Interrogation and interviewing are rather like baking a pie or building a house: What you get out of it is what you put into it. If your attitude is controlled by your opinion, then you might not think defense or resistance is natural, and this alone is the greatest single impediment that causes poor interrogation among some enforcement officers.

Although the directions are parallel and many times the backgrounds are similar, the end goals of the private and commercial security sectors may differ from those of law enforcement in that security is concerned with securing the corporate assets. It may involve using enforcement procedures, but it does with certainty cause law-enforcement attitudes in the private and commercial sectors. We have never really felt that there is a simple answer to anything, perhaps only simple people, but if we were to oversimplify, the most important attitudes that we, as interviewers/interrogators, have to develop are:

1. That we are searching for truths (based on *adequate* investigative preparation).

2. That we have a sincere belief in what we are doing.

3. That we have insight into and awareness of our human emotions and emotional reaction.

4. That we are sensitive to the emotional structure of others.

5. That we shall always attempt to preserve and never deliberately destroy the human dignity of another.

6. That our prime purpose is that we are trying to resolve issues (and this means helping and giving, as opposed to taking).

B. INSIGHT AND AWARENESS

One cannot fully obtain the attitudes that we have described unless one is aware, with some degree of insight, of one's own bias (bias is just an opinion, perhaps unpopular but still an opinion). We have not room here to describe, nor lifetimes to research, all of the biases that the human is capable of; therefore, we would ask that one objectively do some "soul searching" and look at himself.

What are your biases as they relate to the world and your job? Are you a little skeptical about yourself? Should you not be a little skeptical about yourself? Are there others that you dislike on sight? Are there some others whose acts you find so heinous as to be totally indefensible? Do you recognize that even the most carefully thought out judgment arrived at by the process of rationalization is still just bias?

There is an old Gnostic saying, "Good and evil are horns on the same goat." If you can examine this area of yourself and the attitudes subsequently formed from it, then you may have a point of reference toward this insight and awareness that we speak of. All we can seek to do is aid you in gaining a perspective; you must find your own frame of reference.

C. BIASES OR PREJUDICES

1. Harmful

As stated earlier, we cannot take the time to point up all human biases, but those that we have seen which most commonly hinder the interrogator will be enumerated and discussed:

a. The Bias of Overcompensation

By this time, you will have become so critical of your own prejudice structure that you should be made aware that

the pendulum swings in two directions and it becomes perfectly possible for one to say to one's self, "I shall
compensate for my bias by adding on the other end," and
this, of course, can produce a situation more harmful than
the original bias. A wise philosopher once said: "The only
way to accept the teachings of others, including my own
teaching, is with moderation." We urge this same approach
to our readers.

b. Race

c. Creed.

d. Sex.

e. Size (weight, height, etc.)

f. Education.

g. Religion.

h. Geographic origin.

i. Economic status.

j. Deviant behavior.

2. Helpful.

If we were all reduced to the primal state, it would be very easy
to recognize enemies; such as, animals not of our species or
situations leading to great danger or another of our species in
trouble. Because of evolution and the complexity of social
structure, we tend to lose sight of our primitive responsibilities,
especially toward another of our species in trouble. Yet, this is
probably the basic method of combating harmful bias—an
attitude, a belief, a philosophy, and a true in-depth feeling that
"I like people." If you cannot develop the attitude or philosophy that "I like people," or have a basic respect for another's
philosophy and posture, then you will never achieve even
adequacy as an interviewer/interrogator.

There is a paradox that comes from being an extention of
authority, whether it be civil or corporate, and these quotes

(from *Concerning Dissent and Civil Disobedience*, by Abe Fortas, published by the The New American Library, Copyright 1968, page 9) certainly sum up that paradox: The Paradox: The Duty to Obey and to Disobey:

"Obedience to law is the only path to Freedom." *A Passim Proverb*

"I think that we should be men first and subjects afterward." *Thoreau*

"... liberty is to be free from restraint and violence from others, which cannot be where there is no law." *John Locke*

"... law is restraint and absence of restraint is anarchy." *Benjamin Cardozo*

"Human history began with an act of disobedience—it is likely to end with an act of obedience." *Erich Fromm*

This paradoxical quality involves taking a position after much self-examination, and that is what we are asking you to do: Examine yourself beyond the basic needs of food, clothing, shelter, sex, reproduction, recognition, etc., and see how you relate to other humans.

D. CIVIL LIBERTIES

For some time, we have listened to people who criticized the U.S. Supreme Court in rendering the Miranda and other similar decisions as being harmful to law enforcement, as if this were a new interpretation of law. The fact is that the Miranda and other related decisions are not new, but merely a reaffirmation of what federal enforcement agents have followed since 1787.

Although federal statutes make it a crime to knowingly deprive anyone of his civil liberties, we are not aware of any case in which a law-enforcement officer was prosecuted under these statutes for obtaining a false confession. The courts have taken the attitude that a false confession is similar to the fruits of a crime, and this would seem to be the only safeguard against false confessions' getting into evidence.

Our civil liberties are guaranteed by the Constitution, which is protective of the individual and certainly points out that society has no rights. Any who espouse the question, "What about the rights of society?" are creating a false dichotomy and running themselves around in circles.

It is our view that interviewing and interrogation in a true, persuasive, amiable setting in no way deny, nor should deny, any civil liberties, and that any person who steps out of these constitutional bounds may be in violation of the statutes protective of civil liberties, and that he should in fact be subject to the full scrutiny of the judicial process for any such infraction.

The mere fact that an interviewer/interrogator is not a law-enforcement officer should not afford him a protective shield from having his conduct scrutinized by judicial process. We have been made aware of many violations of civil liberties by private citizens in the private and commercial security sectors. It is just a matter of time before the courts recognize that the private and commercial sectors, which have begun to professionalize, have many of the same areas of authority as the law-enforcement officer. To exempt the private and commercial security sectors from the same restrictive legislation as the law-enforcement officer, seems ludicrous indeed. The very safeguards that are constitutionally available to restrain enforcement officers from abuses are not as easily available to protect us from abuses in the private and commercial security sectors.

E. STANDARDS AND PROFESSIONALISM

Somehow the interrogator is ashamed of his art. There seems to be a general public abhorrence of the word "interrogation" as synonymous with third degree, psychological abuse, etc. Even the enforcement officer has given tacit approval of this illusion by removing the work "interrogation" from his vocabulary in some jurisdictions and substituting "interviewing."

The interrogator is not an inquisitor; he is serving a useful purpose completely consistent with our judicial system. His usefulness is even more increased if he is a disinterested professional. Even in law enforcement, the interviewer/interrogator should not be the arresting officer or any person who has any subtle interest or emotional involvement. As the interviewer/interrogator depends upon specialized aides, such as the polygraphist, the psychologist, or the psychiatrist, so the general investigator should come to regard the interviewer/interrogator as a specialist.

The interviewer/interrogator is, in fact, a specialist having an acquired skill. He should be professionally accountable to law, and we would hope that eventually there will be some form of licensing for professional practitioners of this art, especially in the private and commercial sectors.

F. PROFESSIONAL ETHICS OF INTERVIEWING AND INTERROGATION

1. Responsibility

Responsibility has two meanings.

a. The first meaning is that only responsible persons should practice the art of interviewing/interrogation.

We have set moral and ethical standards for the men and women who treat our bodies and minds. We have set moral and ethical standards for the men and women who try our laws. We have even made attempts to set moral and ethical standards for the enforcers of our laws. Surely, there should be some guideline of moral and ethical standards for specialists in the art of interviewing and interrogation, for nowhere are the personal ethics of the practitioner more important and less accountable than in this field.

We note that false confessions are inadmissible, but to this date we know of no law enforcement officer who has ever been prosecuted for unethically taking a false statement in any form. In our view, therefore, the professional interviewer/interrogator should demonstrate mature judgment. All of the social guidelines used to ascertain maturity and strength of character in the other professions should come to focus in selecting candidates for professional interviewing/interrogation.

To take a teen-aged, recently employed clerk and suddenly give this person a life or death power in the job interview is tantamount to a criminal act. It certainly bespeaks no moral judgment on the part of the corporate bodies that allow such transgressions. The importance of selecting a responsible person to handle the secret and private life of another human being is obvious.

We would hope that most of our enforcement candidates, in and of themselves, are morally responsible people. Just as there is a distinction in law enforcement assigned to investigator as opposed to patrolman or guard, so there should be a distinction assigned to interviewer/interrogator as opposed to investigator. All things come back to a morally responsible person.

b. The second meaning of responsibility is the very meaning of law itself: that we are responsible for our own acts.

All interviewers/interrogators should, therefore, keep adequate records of interviews/interrogations. All reports and statements should be maintained for at least a ten-year period. All interviews and interrogations should be accompanied by time logs, which are also maintained for a ten-year period. The interviewer/interrogator should be made legally responsible for the maintenance of such records.

The interviewer/interrogator should be made legally responsible also for safeguarding the rights of the individual beyond legal inadmissibility of false statements; that is, if someone elicits a false confession or violates someone's rights in obtaining a fraudulent confession, then he should be subject to some prosecutive action. There should be a method of auditing and upgrading the actions of interviewers/interrogators, perhaps in the form of a professional association devoted to safeguarding the ethics and standards of professionalism.

One method of assuring responsibility of action would be the maintaining and preserving of audio records of all interviews and interrogations, no matter who conducted them. This, in fact, might well be an excellent goal for a professional group to seek.

2. Individuality

Although there are rules that we have set up as guidelines for interviewing/interrogation, no two interviews or interrogations are alike. Yet, legal scrutiny may not treat the results of interviews/interrogations with this individual attention.

Once a person says to you, the interviewer/interrogator, I have committed (an act), then you, the interviewer/interrogator, cannot disclaim responsibility for that individual. You have formed an interpersonal link with him and must be responsible for preserving the individual nature of that person as it relates to his statement.

For example, seldom are extenuating circumstances included in a confession or statement of fact. Yet, to be perfectly fair and prevent the law from taking on a Juggernaut quality, it is incumbent upon the interviewer/interrogator to elicit these facts as well and to make sure they also are presented along with any admissions against self-interest.

3. Goals

The interviewer/interrogator should have an educational level or background and experience that would equate to a bachelaureate degree. There should be a constant striving toward improvement of the state of the art. A professional association should be formed to implement all that we have discussed.

4. Profile

There should be a profile of the professional interviewer/interrogator. As a starting point, we should like to present such a model of the interviewer/interrogator as a person having a bachelor's degree or its equivalent. If we are referring to someone in law enforcement, then the bachelor's degree could be supplanted by five years of investigative experience. The person should have served an internship with an experienced interviewer/interrogator; we believe six months to be an adequate time.

Within the background training of the interviewer/interrogator, we should like to see courses in ethics, law, logic, evidence, psychology, abnormal psychology, personnel management, public speaking, investigative technique, and even dramatics. A course in report writing should also be prerequisite.

Whatever you do as an interviewer/interrogator is volitional on your part, and the strongest judge and jury to which you will ever have to be responsible is you, yourself. The knowledge of this can never be erased, and no matter how you try to rationalize, you do hold another's most private possession, his private, secret life, his innermost being, in your hands when you interview or interrogate.

We hope most fervently that those who read this book shall be most aware of this awesome responsibility and shall endeavor to follow the creed of the interviewer/interrogator, which is *not* "I have gotten a confession" or "I have destroyed another human being," but rather, "I have helped another human being to resolve an immediate conflict."

APPENDICES

A. Pre-Interview Checklist

B. Sample Statements

    1. Opening Paragraphs

    2. Checklist for Content

    3. Closing Paragraphs

    4. Script for Oral Statements

C. Sample Resignations

D. Interview Information, Including Time Log

E. Tape Recorded Interview Control Sheet

A. Pre-Interview Checklist

Subject_____ Primary objective _____

Physical Description_____ Collateral objective_____

Pertinent Financial Background_____

_____

Known Employment Background_____

_____

_____

Pertinent Personal Matters_____

_____

_____

Hostility Background_____

Police Record_____

Insubordination Record_____

Reputation for Violence_____

Reputation for Aggression_____

Reputation for Passivity_____

Exhibition of Guilt Symptoms_____

Evidence Against_____ Source_____

_____   _____

_____   _____

_____   _____

Information Against_____   _____

_____   _____

_____   _____

_____   _____

B. 1. Opening Paragraphs

I, _____ am aware that _____ is an agent of _____. I wish to voluntarily furnish the following information regarding _____. I make this statement of my own free will and give it in good faith.

I, _____ wish to furnish a free and voluntary statement to _____ whom I know to be _____. I am aware that I have a right to remain silent, that anything contained in this statement can be used against me in a court of law or public hearing, that I may have an attorney present and that if I cannot afford a lawyer a court will provide one for me. I wish to make this statement in good faith because it is the truth to the best of my knowledge.

The following statement concerns my _____ in _____, which occurred _____. I am aware that this statement concerns a matter that is against my interest but I wish to state all the facts freely and in good faith so that the truth may be known. I furnish this statement to _____ whom I know to be _____. I know that this statement could cost me _____ but I want the facts to be known. I am aware that this statement will be used in some form of public hearing.

B. 2. Checklist for Content

1. Beginning date and time
2. Description of locale and persons present
3. Waiver of Rights
   A. Right to remain silent
   B. Anything said can and will be used against interest
   C. Right to have an attorney present
   D. Knowledge that if indigent a court will provide counsel
   E. Demonstrated understanding of above rights
   F. Knowledgeable waiver
   G. Education
   H. Language fluency
4. Synopsis of main admission against interest (first focus of reader's attention)
5. Detail of main admission
   A. What
   B. When
   C. Where
   D. How
   E. Who
   F. With whom
   G. Why
6. Testing assertion of main admission
7. Cross examination regarding main admissions believability.
8. Synopsis of collateral admissions
9. Detail of collateral admissions
10. Testing believability of collateral admissions (fruits of the crime)
11. Awareness of need to compensate victim and subsequent payback by violator to society, victim, or insurance company.

12. Voluntary quality
13. Ending date and time

B. 3. Closing Paragraphs

I have read and corrected this statement which I furnished freely and willingly.

_____
Date
Time

I have read the foregoing statement and initialed all additions, corrections and errors, attesting that this statement is the truth to the best of my knowledge and belief.

_____
Date
Time

The foregoing statement concerning _____ is the truth to the best of my knowledge and belief. I have corrected all errors and additions and have placed my initials at those points. I have read the statement and it is the truth to the best of my knowledge.

_____
Date
Time

B. 4. Script for Oral Statement

Q: Are you aware that this is a tape recorder and that we are recording this conversation?

A:

Q: Do you object to having your conversation with me recorded?

A:

Q: How far did you go in school?

A:

Q: Can you understand the English language?

A:

Q: Can you read and write the English language?

A:

Q: We have decided that it suits our purposes to merely record our conversation rather than to go into a written statement. Is that agreeable with you?

A:

Q: (lead into opening paragraph or declaration of rights).

C. Sample Resignations

I wish to resign my job at _____effective immediately.

_____
Date

For personal reasons I wish to quit my job at _____. This resignation is to become effective _____.

_____
Date

For personal reasons I wish to resign my job with _____. Nothing in this resignation implies that I participated in any illegal act. This resignation is to become effective _____.

_____
Date

D. Interview Information Including Time Log

Subject_____   Date_____   Time_____

Address_____   Interviewer_____

Phone_____ Age_____   D.O.B._____ Witness_____

Occupation_____   Tenure____ Interpreter_____

Marital Status_____   Dependents_____

Financial Data_____

_____

_____

Time Key Phrasing_____

_____
_____
_____
_____
_____
_____
_____
_____
_____
_____
_____
_____
_____
_____
_____
_____
_____

Statement started_____ Statement ended____Interview Concluded_____

E. Tape Recorded Interview Control Sheet

CLIENT: _____

CASE NO: _____ DATE OF INTERVIEW: _____

SUBJECT: _____

INTERVIEWERS: _____
_____

LOCATION OF INTERVIEW: _____

TIME INTERVIEW BEGAN: _____ FINISHED: _____

TAPING RESPONSIBILITY: _____ DATE: _____

_____ DATE: _____

TRANSCRIBED BY: _____ DATE: _____

_____ DATE: _____

TRANSCRIPTION CERTIFIED BY: _____ DATE: _____

FINAL DRAFT TYPED BY: _____ DATE: _____

FINAL DRAFT PROOFED BY: _____ DATE: _____

TAPE ENTERED IN LOG BY: _____ DATE: _____

INDEX

A

Accusation, making, 204
Acquiescence, 122-128
Addenda to statement, 211-212
Address cards, 98
Admissibility, 158, 161-162
Admission, first, 143
Admissions and confessions, 164-168
Age, 77-78
Aids and auxiliaries, 55-56
Alcohol, 74-75
Alibi, 163
Amphetamine, 75
Amplification of guilt, 136-139
Anger, 81-82
Appearance:
    interviewer, 30
    job applicant, 63
Arrest records, criminals, 97
Arrogance, 67
Assertions, test, 102-103, 185
Association, principles, 86-87
Atonement, need, 135-136
Attitude, 30, 219-221
Attitude questions, 35-36
Auxiliaries, aids and, 55-56
Awareness, 221

B

Background information, 53, 56
Bailey, F. Lee, 181
Barbiturates, 75
Believability, statement, 192
Biases:
    harmful, 221-222

Biases *(cont.)*
    helpful, 222-223
    psychological factor, 89
Birth records, 98
Bluffs, 64, 68, 146
Bond, persons and acts coverable, 202-204
Bonding insurance, 191
Brainwashing, 24
Breakthrough:
    bluff, 146
    "buy signs," 144-146
        bypassed, 144
        capitalize, 145-146
        denying allegation not mentioned,
            144
        "ego sealing," 144-145
        most common, 144
        physiological link between right
            arm and deception, 144
        variables, 144
        "Yes" attitude or mood, 144
    defined, 143-144
    first admission, 143
    furnishing relief, 146-148
        inducing stress, 147
        just prior to breakthrough, 147
        question produces threat, 146
        sense of fairness, 148
        sense of order, 148
        "Taking wind out of their sails,"
            147-148
        verbalizing defenses before prospect,
            148
    overconditioning, 150-151
        aid subject's psychological readjust-
            ment, 151
        diminished returns, 150
        false confession, 150

Breakthrough
    overconditioning *(cont.)*
        original concepts of reality dis-
            torted, 150
        uncorroborated testimony, 150
    psychological moment, 128
    re-establishing stress, 148-150
        "conditioned reflex," 149
        lines or levels of defense, 149
        pattern of psychological depen-
            dence, 148
Burden of proof, 163
Business, regular entries, 170
"Buy signs," 144-146 (*see also* Break-
    through)

C

Caffeine, 76
Capability, 159
Character, appraising, 53
Character defamation, 96
Children, 77-78
Cigarettes, 74
Circumstantial evidence, 53, 156-157
City directories, 53
Civil liberties, 223-224
Clues, 101-102
Cocaine, 75
Co-conspirators, 208-211
Coffee, 76
Color-blindness, 84-85
Commercial interview, 176
Communication, 31
Competency, 160-161
Complex questions, 34-35
Complex statement, components, 179-180
Compliance, 122-128
Compromise, 67
Concerning Dissent and Civil Disobedience,
    223
Conclusions, 103-104
Conditioned reflex, 83, 147, 149
Conditioning:
    organism, 23, 24
    over, 150-151
Conduct, 30
Confessions, 82, 115-116, 125-127, 164-
    168, 190-215 (*see also* Proof of
    loss)
Confidence, suspect's, 119, 121
Confidential sources and informants, 51
Confirmation, request, 98
Contemptuous attitudes, 68-69
Continuity, 194, 195
Contraband, 56

Control, attempts to seize, 66-67
Corrections, 184
Corroboration, 178, 184
Court records, 98
Credit rating data, 98
Crime insurance claim, 189
Criminal record, 53, 97
Cross-examination:
    ask about known as if unknown, 44
    ask about unknown as if known, 44
    compare known facts with subject's
        statements, 45
    explaining away damaging evidence, 45
    have subject repeat testimony, 43
    inquiries and interviews, 100-101
    never loud, abusive, or "third degree,"
        43
    pointing out physical signs of lying, 45
    rationalize with subject, 45
    suggestive questions and inferences, 44
    summarize known facts, 45
    vague or evaded sections of testimony
        or confessions, 44-45

D

Dauber, 85
Death records, 98
Deception, 25, 90-91, 103, 111, 134
Defamation of character, 96
Defense:
    lines or levels, 149
    reduction, 134
Dependence, psychological, 148
Derogatory information, 22, 23
Direct evidence, 156
Direct examination, 41-42
Directories, 53
Discerning questions, 33
Drugs, 75-76
Dying declaration, 169-170

E

"Ego sealing," 144-145
Elderly, 77-78, 87
Electronic recordings, 177
Emotional inroads:
    father or respected figure image, 133-
        134
    normal personality insecurity, 135-139
        insecurity or guilt feeling amplifica-
            tion, 136-139
        need for expiration, 135-136
Emotional types, 125

Emotions, 81-83 (*see also* Psychological factors)
Empathy, interviewer, 66
Employment interviews, pre-, 106-108
Employment records, 98
Escape by confessing, 82
Ethics:
    goals, 227
    individuality, 226-227
    profile, 227
    responsibility, 225-226
Evidence:
    admissibility and weight, 158
    background information, 53
    burden of proof, 163
    classifications, 155-158
        ancient times, 155
        circumstantial, 156-157
        direct, 156
        no universal rules, 156
        physical, 157-158
    competency and incompetency, 160-161
        evidence, 160
        witnesses, 160-161
    hearsay rule, 163-171
        confessions and admissions, 164-168
        conversations in presence of defendant, 169
        dying declarations, 169-170
        former testimony, 171
        matters of pedigree, 171
        public records, 170
        regular entries in course of business, 170
        Res Gestae declaration, 170
        tacit admissions, 168-169
    judicial notice, 162-163
    materiality and immateriality, 159-160
    other tests of admissibility, 161-162
    relevancy and irrelevancy, 158-159
    rules, 103-104
    summary, 171
Excitement, neutral, 82-83
Expert examinations, 56
Expiation, need, 135-136
Expressions, 30
Extended answer questions, 33
Extra-judicial confessions, 166
Eye defects, 84-85

F

Father image, 133-134
Fatigue, 76

Fear-reducing statements, 63
Fears, 82, 107, 108, 109, 122, 123, 124
Females, 66-67, 78, 110-111
Fidelity insurance claim, confession supporting, 190-215 (*see also* Proof of loss)
Fifth Amendment, 171
"Fight or flight mechanism," 91
Firmness, interviewer, 66-67
Formality, 62-64
Former testimony, 171
Fortas, Abe, 223
Free narrative, 41, 99, 120
Free-narrative statement:
    first person, 180
    impeached, 180, 181
    limits hearsay quality, 180
    not words of subject, 181
Fulfillment, desire, 136

G

Goals, 227
"Guilt drives," 123
Guilt feeling amplification, 136-139
"Guilt" symptoms, 83

H

Habit, 83
Hallucinogens, 75
Head injury, 87
Hearsay information, 52
Hearsay rule and exceptions, 163-171 (*see also* Evidence)
Hostility, 53, 61, 62-64
Hunger, 76-77

I

Immateriality, 159-160
Impartiality, interviewer, 66
Impeachment, 52, 180, 181
Incompetency, 160-162
Inconsistencies, 102
"Incriminating statement," 165
Individuality, 226-227
Inferences, 103-104
Influence, 30
Injury, head, 87
Inquiries and interviews:
    appropriate pretext, 98
    attempts to evade question, 102
    authority, 95
    clues of additional information, 101-102

Inquiries and interviews *(cont.)*
  conflicting information, 102
  cross-examination, 100-101
    close of interview, 101
    controlling witness, 101
    distorted, misleading or vague
        statements, 100
    dying declaration, 101
    literal written record, 101
    nervous tension and forgetting, 100
    not with friendly witness, 100
    relative value of information, 101
    separate lies from mistakes, 100
    subsequent interviews, 101
    test completeness or accuracy of
        testimony, 100
    test or confirm information, 100
  custodians of records, 97
  explore "unknown details," 99-100
    direct examination, 100
    failure to ask key questions, 99-100
    free-narrative discussion, 99
    sequence of questions and answers,
        99
    starting interview, 99
    unimportant questions, 100
  give reasons for inquiries, 96
  inconsistencies, 102
  interview, term, 95
  neighbors, general public, 98
  officials or organizations, 98
  personal, face-to-face, 98
  pre-employment, 106-108
  pre-promotional, 109
  qualifying embarrassing answers, 100,
      105
  request for confirmation, 98
  results, 103-104
    facts admissible under rules of evi-
        dence, 103
    false assumptions, 104
    interpreting facts, 104
    relevant and material, 103
    time to evaluate, 103
  revealing identity, 98
  showing credentials, 98
  specific topics, 99
  systems and operational, 109-110
  test assertions, 102-103
    how information was obtained, 102
    play "Devils Advocate," 103
    reliability of witness, 102-103
    separate facts from opinions, 103
    witness who lies from habit, 103
  transfer, 109
  unfriendly witnesses, 104-106

Inquiries and interviews
  unfriendly witnesses *(cont.)*
    changing topic, 106
    cooperation, 105
    exaggerating facts, 105
    motivate, 105
    overcoming excuses, 105
    positive leading questions, 105
    quarrelsome, 106
    reasons, 104
    retain control of subject's "submis-
        sion," 105
    second investigator present, 106
    self-secure feeling, 105
    stating information out of context,
        105
    subpoenaed, 106
    surreptitious recording, 106
    unobjectionable information, 104
  uninvolved, disinterested persons, 97
  vague answers, 102
  witness, 95-97, 99 *(see also* Witness)
  women, 110-111
Insanity, 163
Insecurity:
  formation, 147
  insecurity or guilt feeling amplification,
      136-139
  need for expiation, 135-136
Insight, 221
Instruments of crime, 56
Insured, the, 191
Interpreter, 46-47
Interrogation:
  consolidate accomplishments, 128-129
  encourage acquiescence and pursue
        indicators of compliance, 122-
        128
  investigative processes, 51
  make submission tolerable, 122
  nothing pleasurable, 146
  offer mutually acceptable solution, 121
  pre-, 116-119
  suspects of questionable guilt, 129-130
  undermine suspect's confidence of suc-
        cess, 119-121
  why suspects confess, 115-116
Interrogatories, 196-198
Interview log and notes, 177-178
Interviewer, image, 65-69
Interviewing and interrogation:
  "brainwashing," 24
  deception, 25
  derogatory information, 22, 23
  determining objective, 54
  do's and don'ts, 23

Interviewing and interrogation *(cont.)*
  emotional inroads, 24
  ethics, 225-228
  exploration and resolution of issues, 25
  formalized guide for application of
      rules, 23
  how to interrogate, 115-130 *(see also*
      Interrogation)
  innate skill and sufficient experience,
      23
  inquiries and interviews, 95-111 *(see
      also* Inquiries and interviews)
  interrogation, definition, 21
  interview, definition, 21
  intuition, 23
  job applicants rejected, 22
  legal system, 24
  location, 56-58 *(see also* Location)
  meaningful systematic persuasion, 24-
      25
  order of interviewing, 64
  organism conditioning, 23, 24
  physical and mental influence factors,
      23
  practice, 23
  pre-employment polygraph testing, 22
  puritanical social orientation, 22
  rights of individual, 24, 25
  self-interest, 22
  stress, 24
  systematized study, 23
  terms used interchangeably, 21
  understanding behavior, 22
  what's missing in current practice, 21-
      23
Intoxicated persons, 167
Intuition, 23
*Investigation and Preparation of Criminal
    Cases Federal and State,* 181
Investigation reports, 53
Irrelevancy, 158-159

J

Job interviewing, 106-108
Judicial confession, 165-166
Judicial notice, 162-163

K

Karpman, 123

L

Labels, question-and-answer format, 181
Laboratory examinations, 56

Language, 29
Leading questions, 33-34, 193-194
Legal system, 24
Lineup, 56
Liquor, 74-75
Listening, surreptitious, 51
Location:
  comfortable, 57
  decrease subject's fears, 57
  distracting influences, 57
  distracting movements, 58
  exclude friends and relatives, 57
  friendly witnesses, 56
  image of interviewer, 57
  keep subject from viewing accident
      scene, 58
  moving, 56
  no glaring lights, 57
  no signs of restraint, 57
  on-the-scene, 58
  pictures, 58
  pre-interview defensiveness, 57
  private, 57
  removed from familiar surroundings,
      56
  seat the subject, 58
  strange to subject, 56
  telephones excluded, 58
  unshaded windows, 58
Log, interview, 177-178
Lying:
  habit, 103
  interviewer, 65
  psychological factor, 90-91
  women, 111

M

Management applicant, 108
Marriage records, 98
Materiality and immateriality, 159-160
Mechanics of questioning, 29-47 *(see also*
    Questioning, mechanics)
Memory, 86-87 *(see also* Psychological
    factors)
Miranda, 223
Motive, 159

N

Negatives, double or triple, 34
Nervousness, interviewer, 69
Neurosis, 135
Neutral excitement, 82-83
Neutrality, interviewer, 66
Non-directive approach, 137-138

Nostalgia, 134
Notary, 180, 184
Notes, interview, 177

O

Objective, interviewing and interrogation,
    21, 54 (see also Interviewing and
    interrogation)
Old people, 77-78, 87
Openmindedness, interviewer, 66
Operational interviewing, 109-110
Opiates, 75
Opportunity, 159
Order of interviewing, 64
Organism conditioning, 23, 24
Overconditioning, 150-151

P

Parental image, 133-134
Pedigree, matters of, 71
Pell, Arthur R., 106
Perception, 84-85
Personnel interviews, 176
Personality, interviewer, 64, 65
Photographs, 56
Physical evidence, 53, 157-158
Physical influence factors:
    age, 77-78
        children, 77-78
        old people, 78
    alcohol, 74-75
    coffee and tea (caffeine), 76
    drugs, 75-76
    fatigue, 76
    hunger and thirst, 76-77
    introductory statement, 73
    sex, 78
    smoking, 74
Positive positioning, 137
Practice, 23
Precise questions, 32-33
Pre-employment interviewing, 106-108
Pre-interrogation, 116-119
Pre-interview:
    checklist, 231
    dress or physical appearance, 63
    exhibited formality and hostility, 61,
        62-64
    fear-reducing statements, 63
    feeling of formality, 61
    inefficient spontaneous inquiries, 63
    interview differs from interrogation, 63
    interviewer, 65-69
        antagonizing the subject, 69

Pre-interview
    interviewer (cont.)
        arrogance, 67
        attempts to seize control, 66-67
        compromise, 67
        contemptuous attitudes, 68-69
        display total confidence, 69
        empathy, 66
        evaluate each development, 68
        female applicants, 66-67
        firmness, 66-67
        gentleness, 69
        impartiality, 66
        keep open mind, 67
        listening, 69
        mentality or physical endurance of
            subject, 68
        not prejudge, 67
        not try to impress subject, 68
        patience, 69
        persistence, 69
        personality, 64, 65
        raising your voice, 69
        search for truth, 69
        self-discipline, 67-69
        signs of nervousness, 69
        sincerity, 65
        staged events or bluffs, 64, 68
        subdue personal prejudices, 67
        sympathy, 65
    order, 64
    proper planning and preparation, 63
    rapport, 61-62
    skepticism and reserve, 61
    sufficient time, 64
    traits, 64
    voluntary witness, 64
Prejudice, 67, 89, 221-223 (see also Biases)
Preparatory work:
    aids and auxiliaries, 55-56
    background information, 53, 56
    defining unknowns, 51-55
    location of interview, 56-58
    processes for procuring information, 51
    unknown details, 54, 55
Pre-promotional interviewing, 109
Pressures, 108
Pride, 127
Principal, 191
Professionalism, 224-225
Profile, 227
Projection, 66
Promotional interviewing, pre-, 109
Proof of loss:
    addenda to statement, 211-212
    confession supporting fidelity insur-
        ance claim, 190-191

Proof of loss *(cont.)*
  confirmation of statement's validity, 204-208
  documenting long term theft situation, 198-201
  duty to repay, 212-215
  establishing, 191-193
  framing lead question, 193-194
  introduction, 189-190
  making an accusation, 204
  objectives, 190
  outside co-conspirators, 208-211
  persons and acts coverable by bond, 202-204
  sample interrogatories that establish recoverable value, 196-198
  tailor statement to meet objective, 202
  what statement must establish to substantiate, 194-196
Psychological factors:
  bias, 89
  deception, 90-91
  emotions, 81-83
    anger, 81-82
    conditioned reflex, 83
    emotional conditions of body, 83
    escape by confessing, 82
    habit, 83
    neutral excitement, 82-83
    physical symptoms, 83
  "fight or flight mechanism," 91
  importance, 81
  memory, 86-87
    first contacts, 86
    head injury, 87
    imagined material, 87
    incidents eliciting strong emotion, 86
    intention to remember, 87
    older people, 87
    principles of association, 86-87
    repeatedly taking testimony, 86
    sensory organs, 87
    time, 86
    vague clues, 86
  perception, 84-85
  recognition, 87-88
  submission, 89-90
  suggestion, 88-89
Public records, 170
Punishment, 123

Q

Question and answer statements:
  balky witness, 181

Question and answer statements *(cont.)*
  each question and answer treated individually, 180
  formal in appearance, 181
  handwriting of witness, 181
  labels, 181
  last form of written statement, 179
  stenographic record, 181
  typewritten, 181
  unwieldy, 181
Questioning, mechanics:
  attitude, 30
  characteristics of good questions, 32-33 (*see also* Questions)
  communication, 31
  composition of questions, 31-47
  conduct and appearance, 30
  cross-examination, 42-45
  direct examination, 41-42
  free narrative, 41
  important types of questions, 33-41 (*see also* Questions)
  influence, 30
  interpreter, use, 46-47
  language or speech, 29
  questions are tools, 31-32
  timing, 52
  words and expressions, 30
  working tools, 29-30
Questions:
  attitude, 35-36
  avoid frightening words, 32
  clear, easily understood, 32
  complex, 34-35
  discerning, 33
  "double or triple negatives," 34
  extended answer, 33
  leading, 33-34, 193-194
  precise, 32-33
  reasons, 54
  sequences, 36-41
    controlled-answer questioning techniques, 40-41
    general to specific, 36-37
    more specific estimates of quantities, 38-39
    reaching backward, 37-38
    vague or indefinite description of quantities, 39-40
  short, confined to one topic, 32
  "unknown details," 99-100

R

Rapport, 61-62, 76
Rationale, statement, 192

Rationalizatioń, 139
Real estate record, 98
Reasonableness, statement, 192
Recognition, 87-88
Recordings, 106
Record:
    criminal, 53, 97
    custodians, 97
    public, 170
Recoverable value, 196-198
Recovery, 208-211
Recruiting and Selecting Personnel, 106-
    108
Relevancy, 158-159
Reliability of witness, 102-103
Relief, furnishing, 146, 148
Remorsefulness, 125-126
Repay, duty, 212-215
Reputation, 124
Res Gestae declaration, 170
Resignations, 234
Respected figure image, 133-134
Responsibility, 225-226
Results, interview, 103-104
Retaliation, fear, 124
Rights of individual, 24, 25
Rogerian technique, 137-138
Rothblatt, Henry B., 181
Rules of evidence, 103-104

                        S

Screening interview, 106
Self-defense, 163
Self-discipline, interviewer, 67-69
Self-incrimination, 171
Self-interest, 22
Sense organs, 84
Sequence, question, 36-41, 99-100 (*see also*
    Questions)
Sex, 66-67, 78, 110-111
Sincerity, interviewer, 65
Smoking, 74
Speech, 29
"Squealer," 124
Staged situations, 146
Standards, 224-225
Statement:
    addenda, 211-212
    believability, 192
    checklist for content, 232-233
    closing paragraphs, 233
    commercial interview, 176
    confession, 190-215 (*see also* Proof of
        loss)
    confirmation of validity, 204-208

Statement *(cont.)*
    introduction, 175-176
    not necessarily a confession, 175
    opening paragraphs, 231-232
    oral, 176-178
        corroboration, 177
        electronic recording, 177
        in writing as soon as possible, 177
        information developed from, 178
        interview log and notes, 177-178
        memorandum to file, 178
    personnel interviewing, 176
        script, 233-234
        stenographic notes, 178
        time log, 177-178
        witness, 177
    organized system, 175
    rationale, 192
    reasonableness, 192
    records preserved as given, 175,176
    safeguarding, 185-186
        for future use, 186
        from suspect/subject, 185
    sample, 231-234
    tailor to meet objective, 202
    testing assertions, 185
    tort actions, 176
    types, 176-184
    written, 178-184
        components of complex ones, 179-
            180
        continuous motion pictures, 184
        corrections, 184
        corroboration, 184
        electronic recordings, 184
        free-narrative, 178-184 (*see also*
            Free-narrative statement)
        impeachment, 180, 181
        initials on each page, 184
        insert one or two errors, 184
        limit on later judicial inquiry, 179
        multi-paged, 184
        notary, 180, 184
        question and answer statements,
            179-184 (*see also* Question
            and answer state-
            ments)
        recommended printed form, 181-
            184
        signature, 178, 184
        simple statement of fact, 178
        time page completed, 184
        witness, 184
Stenographic notes, 178, 181
Stipulation, 67
Stress, 24, 136, 148-150

Stubborness, 125
Submission, 89-90, 105, 122
Subpoena, 106
Subrogation, definition, 191
Suggestion, 88-89
Surety, 191
Surreptitious listening, 51
Surveillance, 51
Sympathy, 65, 126
Systems interviewing, 109-110

T

Tacit admissions, 168-169
"Taking the wind out of their sails," 147-
    148
Tea, 76
Telephone directories, 53
Telephone numbers, 98
Testing assertions, 102-103, 185
Theft, long term, 198-201
Thirst, 76-77
Time, 86
Time log, 177-178, 234-235
Tiredness, 76
Tobacco, 74
Tort actions, 176
Traffic records, 97
Tranquilizers, 75
Transfer interviewing, 109
Trial and error, 23

U

Uncorroborated testimony, 150

Undercover, 51
Unknown details, 54, 55, 99-100

V

Vagueness, 102
Validity, 204-208
Value, recoverable, 196-198
Visual limitations, 84-85
Voluntariness, 165

W

Weight, 158
Wharton, 165
Witness:
    abnormal mentality, 96
    arranging interview, 96
    competency, 160
    employee at work, 96
    incentives, 96
    interest and point of view, 96
    interview quickly, 96
    orient, 99
    publicity seekers, 96
    reasons for not giving information,
        96-97
    reliability, 102-103
    time means money, 95
    ulterior personal motives, 96
    unfriendly, 104-106 (*see also* Inquiries
        and interviews)
Women, 66-67, 78, 110-111
Words, 30